BATHROOM BOOK
of
ALBERTA TRIVIA
Weird, Wacky and Wild

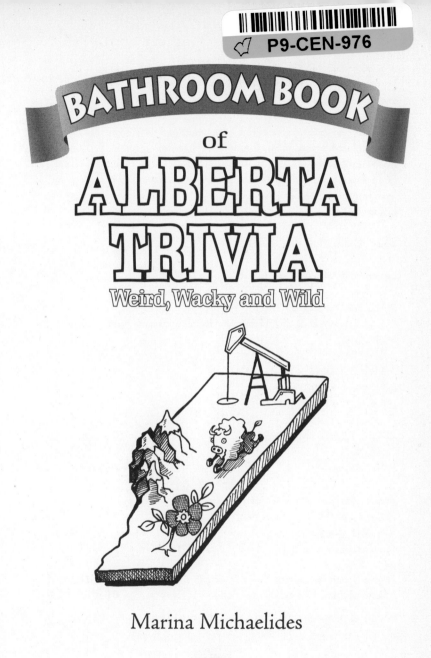

Marina Michaelides

BLUE
BIKE
BOOKS

The Publisher: Blue Bike Books

Library and Archives Canada Cataloguing in Publication

Michaelides, Marina, 1963–
    Bathroom book of Alberta trivia: weird, wacky and wild / Marina Michaelides.

(Bathroom books of Canada; 3)
ISBN-13: 978-0-9739116-2-6
ISBN-10: 0-9739116-2-X

    1.-Alberta—Miscellanea.- I.-Title.

FC3661.M54 2006   971.23   C2006-900317-3

Project Director: Nicholle Carrière
Project Editor: Nicholle Carrière
Cover Image: Roger Garcia
Illustrations: Roger Garcia

Produced with the assistance of the Government of Alberta, **Government** Alberta Multimedia Development Fund **of Alberta** ■

We acknowledge the financial support of the Government of Canada through the Canada Book Fund (CBF) for our publishing activities.

■✦■   Canadian   Patrimoine
        Heritage   canadien

PC: P1

DEDICATION

The world is much lovelier because John is in it—thank you for showing me how and that I may.

And to my wonderful mother, Stella, who is simply adorable, and to my very funny, cheeky and delightful father D.J.

For support and so, so many kisses, thanks Nick, Anna, Yolanda, two Helens, Nicola, Sean, Athena, Daphne, Theo, Bella, K.P.M., my big, mad Greek family and all my friends who graciously put up with my plentiful mistakes.

ACKNOWLEDGEMENTS

To all Albertans, whose genius and humour made this possible. And to Faye, for smiling at me all the time and saying yes in the first place. Nicholle...a thousand thanks for checking and spelling and editing and doing all the things that make writers look good.

CONTENTS

THE LONG ARM OF THE LAW

RECORD BREAKERS

EDMONTON VERSUS CALGARY

CULTURE

SHOPPING

EDUCATION AND HEALTH

SCIENCE AND TECHNOLOGY

THE ECONOMY AND THE GOVERNMENT

ODDS AND ENDS

INTRODUCTION

Collecting trivia is like going grocery shopping—there are way too many temptations to divert you from the task at hand.

You start with the best intentions. You promise yourself to stick to the shopping list, ready to delve into shelves packed with all the essentials—sports, culture, quirky history, a little geography…It comes frozen! Really? Hmm. All these different subjects in the superstore of information. Yum. Where to start? Ah! This aisle.

To begin with, I did get lost. I admit it. In the weather aisle. As a Mediterranean, I have a never-ending fascination with anything to do with freezing cold record temperatures (mostly because I can't believe that as a-five-year permanent resident, I've survived even one of them). Before I knew it, I'd been reading the labels on all the frozen foods (aka records of lowest and highest provincial temperatures) for hours. Stunning! But they were about to close the store on me. All the other shoppers had left. So skip that section unless the natural world of hailstorms, blizzards, floods, tornadoes, droughts and disasters, for you too, is a tantalizing appetizer.

Moving on. I was determined this menu of trivia would be a balanced diet. Back to the shopping list.

Right. The first staple. Basic bread and butter—dealing with Alberta's history. If it's fresh and hot, it's always good, any time of day. So I've cooked up a simple all-day breakfast of how the province's past affects today—just in case you forgot or you never knew. And it's all told with a twist. Because it's not just about the bread, but the jam you put on top. Or-how about a little Albertan birch syrup?

The celebrities aisle was like raiding the cookie counter—so many goodies, but eat too many and you feel sick. Then I really needed some meat, something to chew on and get my teeth into, and that's what it was like digging around for tidbits on the economy and industry.

Actually, the only hard thing about writing this book was chewing on official statistics. Almost gave me indigestion. Deciphering what they really mean and what's been left out, or purposely put in or spun around, just so the numbers say whatever they want them to say. Sorting that out was like rummaging through a box of green beans and discovering some were totally rotten and others crisp and ready to eat. I've cooked up the clean ones and added some sauce.

Near the end of my trip, when I found out that an ingenious Albertan was responsible for inventing a new kind of fitted sheet, it was like stumbling into the store's Belgian handmade chocolate section. Genius! I doubt it will improve my life, but a fact like that, I shall certainly serve up at dinner parties. Other tidbits, I shall put in the pantry, quietly, among all the other tins and packages, and use them later when someone needs to be impressed over cocktails.

The really tough thing about writing a book like this was knowing when to stop. Trivia is addictive, and if you have no discipline, you could end up weighing 300 pounds, you're happy when friends don't call, and you're alone—getting off on the buzz of a new ice cream flavour (meaning the section on mad and massive roadside attractions). So I stopped. But by that time, I'd forgotten what it was that I came in for in the first place.

JUST THE FACTS...

Alberta's Birthday

September 1, 1905.

Alberta's Namesake

The province is named for Princess Louisa Caroline Alberta. She was born in 1848, the fourth daughter of Queen Victoria of England and Prince Albert. Louisa married John Campbell, later appointed Governor General of Canada. When the time came for Campbell to name the North-West Territories in 1882, he chose "Alberta" in his wife's honour for one of the four regions. The others were called Athabasca, Assiniboine and Saskatchewan.

The Canadian Province of Louisiana??

Hypothetically, given the choices available by the princess's name, Alberta could have started life as the province of Louisiana or Carolina instead. But the Americans had already used both for their states. So, Alberta took the prize, but Lake Louise was given the princess's first name, and today is Canada's largest and most visited ski area.

DID YOU  **KNOW?**

Alberta has three nicknames. Use any one you like: the Princess Province, the Energy Province and the Sunshine Province.

Inspirational Namesake—Would You Call Your Kid a Princess?

In Alberta, in 2004, only one baby girl was given the name Louise, two were called Louisa. One child was named Carolina, and Caroline was chosen nine times. There were five Carolyns and one Carolyne. Of all the names chosen for girls, Alba was the closest to anything resembling our namesake's. But, there were seven boy babies named Albert, one Alberto and an Albie.

Alberta's Provincial Motto

Fortis et Liber is the Latin that defines the province. It means strong and free.

Alberta's official emblems are:
Flower: the wild rose
Bird: the great horned owl
(Hmm, together the flower and bird
would make a wonderful tattoo.)
Stone: petrified wood (Now that's a bit harder to draw.)
Tree: the lodgepole pine
Fish: the bull trout
Imagine the ultimate Alberta tattoo now…a trout in a pine tree that grows wild roses, eating petrified wood while being serenaded by an owl. Any other offers?

Official Provincial Colours
Alberta's are blue and gold.

Big Number Four
Alberta comes fourth in Canada in size in terms of both land and forest area. As well, 10% of Canada's population of 30 million lives in Alberta, making it the fourth-largest province by population. (Ontario, Québec and British Columbia have more residents).

Alberta has a legal tartan. The province's unique plaid was enshrined in a 1961 act of legislation. The colours represent the landscape: green for forests, gold for wheat fields, blue for skies and lakes, pink for the wild rose and (duh!) black for the oil and coal industries.

The Length and Breadth of It
- The province covers a total area of 661,000 km², of which 16,796 km² is water.
- The provincial boundaries are marked by the 49° and 60° north latitude lines and the 110° and 120° west longitude lines.
- Alberta measures 1200 kilometres from north to south and 699 kilometres at its widest point east to west.

Alberta's Population

There were 3,236,906 Albertans in 2004. Urbanites make up 80% of the population, while 20% are rural. The province's population hit the 3 million mark in the year 2000.

Alberta's Major Rivers

The province's chief waterways are the Peace River, the North and South Saskatchewan Rivers and the Athabasca River.

Gas Guzzlers

Of all the Canadian provinces, Alberta is tops for greenhouse gas emissions, not surprising since 40% of national greenhouse gases come from the electricity and petroleum industries. Ontario comes in a close second and Québec is third.

Representation

Alberta has 28 seats in the House of Commons and six in the Senate. By the way, the word "commons" does not refer to "commoners," but is in fact the Anglo-Norman word for "communes."

Just a Flat Prairie? Not!!

It's simply not true that Alberta is just a flat, boring, smooth prairie. Topographical features include the foothills of the Rocky Mountains, a place called Hairy Hill, (where bison traditionally shed their hair), Nose Hill, Two Hills, Three Hills and even Kneehills and Hand Hills (a rock formation that looks like a human hand, hence the name).

Alberta's Legal Drinking Age is 18

This is the same as Québec and Manitoba. In all other Canadian provinces and territories, kids have to wait one more year, until they're 19, before they can start knocking back booze.

You Say Buffalo, I Say Bison

You won't find a single buffalo in Alberta. In fact, you won't find one anywhere in North America, because there is no such thing as a North American buffalo—buffalo are only found in Africa and Asia. If it's Albertan, it's a bison, thank you very much. Bison have a unique shoulder hump that sets them apart from buffalo.

Bird Nests

There are 385 species of birds in Alberta; 250 nest here, while the rest just travel through as they migrate. The province also has 90 mammal, 10 amphibian, eight reptile and 59 fish species.

THE BEST

According to David Phillips, senior climatologist for Environment Canada: "In terms of year-round comfort, nobody can beat Alberta's weather."
What does he know? He lives in Toronto. But it's true…
So, no more moaning about climatic negatives.
Let's celebrate the stats!

The Latest-Breaking Weather News

Weather-wise, Alberta rocks the rest of Canada! This shocking conclusion comes courtesy of a 2005 Environment Canada analysis of 30 years' worth of weather data from 150 national weather stations.

Best National Weather!

It's best in the West, say the statistics—the best national weather overall when 70 different weather categories are taken into account, 24 of which are called "comfort indicators." (There's nothing "comfortable" about your eyelashes freezing off, however.)

Blessed with Allegedly Warm Springs

Oh yeah? It dumped 30 centimetres of snow in just one May day in 2004. Ooops. Was that a moan? Really?…Apparently, the province has very warm autumns (Maybe, but fall only lasts for two weeks, and then winter kicks in with a vengeance, right?)…no smog (That's true.)…no freezing rain (So. The cars skidding into each other last year were a figment of my imagination, right?)…light winds…low humidity (It's so dry, your skin ages five years in one!! That's supposed to be comforting?)… tolerable summers (on the summer day the report was published, thermometers read a mere 15°C, and it rained all day long)…and not much snow…really?

No Snow?
Hate to admit it, but it's true. Since 1971, Alberta's 140 centimetres of snowfall per year has actually been the lowest in all of Canada, which averages 201 centimetres nationally.

Proving What a Sunny Province We Are?

☛ Alberta wins top prize for the most sunny days in cold months, with 115. (Is that supposed to make up for frozen eyelashes?)

☛ The province also enjoys the most sunny days overall year round, with 312.

☛ It also ranked second in the fewest snow days each year, with 60 (so how come it snows on picnic days in August?), and…third in the most days having light wind, with 296.

"The combinations make for an unbeatable Canadian climate," *climatologist Phillips says. Well let's invite him to come and live here* *for a while and see.*

Provincial Rankings for Best Overall Weather

1. Albertaaaaagggghhhhhhhh!!! (Yippee. Where's my bikini?)
2. Saskatchewan
3. British Columbia (Ha ha ha ha ha. Well, it didn't make top, did it?)
4. Ontario
5. New Brunswick
6. Prince Edward Island
7. Yukon
8. Nova Scotia
9. Manitoba
10. Northwest Territories
11. Nunavut
12. Newfoundland & Labrador
13. Québec (So, you wanna be independent with *that* weather?)

Alberta's Best and Worst Weather Rankings
Category Rank Value out of 13 places
(all Canadian provinces and territories)

- First place for lowest annual snowfall, with 140 centimetres
- Second place for the most hours per year of sunlight year-round, with 2203 hours per year
- Third place for the most dry days, with 239 days
- Fourth place for the sunniest spring, with 674 hours of sunlight
- Fifth place for the hottest summer, with an average temperature of 21.8°C
- Fifth place for being the warmest year-round, with an average temperature of 1.7°C
- Fifth place for the fewest freezing days, with 203 days
- Seventh place for humidex days above 30°C, with nine days
- Eighth place for the coldest winter, with an average temperature of −19°C

AND NOW FOR THE BAD WEATHER NEWS

Anyone who foretells Alberta weather is either a newcomer or a fool.
Frank Oliver, Canadian Historical Review, 1946

There's also an old saying:
"If you don't like the weather in Alberta, just wait a minute."

The Most Dramatic Temperature Shifts in a Single Day

This was recorded at Pincher Creek on January 6, 1966, and was caused by a chinook wind (a chinook is produced when warm air funnels through the Rockies). Environment Canada's thermometer readings were −24.4°C at 7:00 AM, 0.6°C at 8:00 AM and 21.7°C at 9:00 AM. That's a 46.1°C fluctuation in two hours! By the way, Pincher Creek is allegedly one of the windiest places in Canada.

Freezing When You Get into Bed at Night?

On December 15, 1964, in Red Deer, the temperature with the wind-chill factor was nearly −73°C after two days of blizzards. One thousand head of livestock died and three people froze to death in their sleep when their stoves went out during the night.

Super Ice

Fort Vermilion holds the provincial record for the coldest-ever day, with a temperature of −61.1°C set on January 1,1911. Worldwide, the golden raspberry for the lowest recorded temperature goes to Vostok in the Antarctic with −89°C.

Alberta boasts the world's worst hailstorms. The area known as "Hailstorm Alley" is a triangular-shaped area defined by Red Deer at the apex, and Calgary and Drumheller on the points of the base. This area has the highest number of hailstorms per year in all of Canada and possibly the world. Every year, there are between four and six massive dumps of ice bombs from the sky, compared to three for the rest of the province.

The Worst Hailstorm in Canadian History

Calgary holds the record. On September 7, 1991, a 30-minute downpour resulted in 62,000 insurance claims for property damage totalling $237 million and 54,000 claims of vehicle damage that cost insurers $105 million.

Men Made of Stones

On July 16, 1996, so much hail fell in Calgary that kids made "hailmen" and enjoyed some midsummer tobogganing.

Hail Stops Shops

On July 11, 2004, Edmonton survived a flood and hailstorm that caused over $180 million in damage. West Edmonton Mall was evacuated—30,000 people—and damage there alone was estimated at $7.4 million.

Tourist Tornado

A sudden tornado in Pine Lake on July 14, 2000, ripped through the tents and trailers of holidaymakers, leaving 12 dead and 140 injured. One thousand people were displaced. Winds within the tornado reportedly reached speeds of 300 kilometres per hour and carried baseball-sized hailstones. Result: $30 million in damages.

Biggest Dump of Snow in Summer

Snow has fallen in Alberta in every single month of the year. The largest summer snowfall was also the worst recorded nationally: 118 centimetres on June 29, 1963, at the Livingston Lookout Tower (located just below the 50th parallel at 114° west longitude).

Edmonton's Hour-Long Tornado Terror

Twenty-seven Edmontonians lost their lives on July 31, 1987, the victims of 420-kilometre-per-hour tornado winds that ripped through the city and areas of Strathcona County. The tornado ravaged the area and remained on the ground for an hour. Hundreds were injured, 300 homes were destroyed and $330 million of property damage was incurred.

Alberta has Low Rainfall?

On July 4, 1998, Calgary recorded 43 millimetres of rainfall in six hours, breaking the record set in 1909.

Alberta has the Lowest Snowfall?
A surprise spring blizzard in 1973, with winds of up to 80 kilometres per hour, downed 2300 telephone poles across the province, leaving people without phones for a week. Five hundred Calgary homes were also left without power. Edmonton's worst hit of snow was 46 centimetres in April 1955.

Never Mind the Oil Patch, What About the Ice Patch?

In January 1969, Edmonton's longest period of continuous, icy, awful, horrible, freezing, nightmarish weather went on and on and on for 26 days, with an average temperature of –17.8°C. The horror finally ended on February 2, but not before one day of killer low –39.4°C that burst half the pipes in the city.

DID YOU KNOW?

The hottest day on record in Alberta is 43.3°C, shared by Brooks, which hit that high in July 1931, and Fort Macleod, which hit the same high a decade later in July 1941.

World and Canadian Sizzlers

The world's highest temperature was recorded on September 22, 1922, in El Aziza, Libya—58°C in the shade! The Canadian record is a mere 45°C, noted at Midale and Yellowgrass, Saskatchewan, in 1937.

Water Shortage

In Grande Prairie, on May 28, 1972, the city engineer advised residents to "drink beer" when water ran out during a summer heat wave. Continuous 40°C temperatures for weeks, coupled with the breakdown of a pump at the water treatment plant, left residents parched.

Thundering Down the Mountain
Tons of snow cascading down was the last thing seven skiers ever saw in 1955 when a massive avalanche rumbled down on them from Mount Temple near Lake Louise. Another avalanche in 1990 in Banff National Park killed four cross-country skiers.

DID YOU  KNOW?

The foothills of the Rocky Mountains see the most rain in all of Alberta and more thunderstorms than anywhere else in Canada.

Waiting for Wesults of the Worst-Ever Pwovincial Washout

The damage caused by the summer floods of 2005 are still to be assessed but are expected to top the $400 million payout from the Calgary 1991 hailstorm. Spring melt and weeklong torrential rain in the Rockies created havoc as far as Saskatchewan.

In Alberta, the Highwood and Oldman Rivers burst their banks, as did the Bow, which flooded downtown Calgary. The Red Deer River overflowed into its namesake city and also hit homes in Drumheller, where one-third of the city was evacuated and the water flowed at a peak of 1500 m³ per second. Despite a 48-hour "state of emergency" declared on June 25 and 26 in Edmonton, the city wasn't inundated.

It wasn't the first and experts say it won't be the last.

Alberta's Other Worst Water Washouts

1899   In Edmonton, the North Saskatchewan River rose more than 12 metres and flooded the local power station, leaving the city powerless for three weeks.

1915   Floods were caused by the highest-ever recorded spring flows on the North Saskatchewan River in Edmonton, caused by rain and spring.

1974   In north-central Alberta, $10 million in damages resulted from spring flooding.

1981   The city of Edmonton couldn't cope when 56 millimetres of rain fell in less than three hours. Four people died as a result of terrible flooding and mudslides.

1986   Fifteen hundred homes were damaged at a cost of $30 million when a July storm ripped through central Alberta.

1987   In the Upper Peace District, heavy rainfall in late July resulted in floods that caused a 96-car freight train derailment and extensive crop damage.

1988   A June flood at Lesser Slave Lake killed two people and left $15 million worth of havoc in its wake.

1990   Heavy rains from May to July caused damage to farmland, homes and municipalities in Thorsby, Winfield, Calman, Mulhurst and Bentley.

1992   Flooding damaged 50 homes and 3800 residents were evacuated from Peace River when above-average temperatures caused ice on the frozen river to break up and melt.

1997   The Peace was shattered again, and this time 400 people were evacuated and damage totalled $48 million.

All Dried Up

The drought in 1987 was so bad that 10% of Alberta's farmers packed up their plows and got out of the business altogether.

OTHER NATURAL DISASTERS

Sliding to Disaster

The worst natural disaster in Canadian history, in terms of lives lost, was the Frank Slide on April 29, 1903. Seventy-six people were killed at the Frank Mine and surrounding area when the mine's entranceway was covered by 30 million cubic metres of limestone cascading down from the face of Turtle Mountain.

☛ **Rapid rubble**. Three square kilometres of land were buried beneath 14,100 metres of rock in just 90 seconds, blocking the main Crowsnest Pass section of the CPR railway. A further disaster was only narrowly avoided by warning an approaching passenger train, the Spokane Flyer, to stop just in time before it collided with the massive wall of the rock that was blocking the rail line.

☛ **A lucky horse**. A month later, when the mine was re-opened, a horse called Charlie emerged from the rubble. He had survived by eating bark from the timber framing on the mine's walls and ceilings.

☛ **Final closure**. The reasons for the slide remain undetermined, but in 1911, the government declared Turtle Mountain unstable, and the town of Frank was relocated nearby. One hundred people still live there today. The mine itself was finally closed down in 1917 after another explosion and extensive fire. All that remains today is a tourist interpretive centre.

Forests of Fire

In May and June 2002, 1000 firefighters worked to put out forest fires near Conklin, Lac La Biche and Wood Bison in northern Alberta. But 250,000 hectares burned up, and 1550 people were evacuated. Damage was calculated at $22.1 million.

Counting the Cost of Coal

Canada's worst coalmining disaster was the 1914 explosion at the Hillcrest Mine in the Crowsnest Pass. Gas ignited and blasted through a labyrinth of tunnels, killing 189 people.

☛ **Alcohol breath.** For once, an overindulgence in alcohol might have saved a couple of miners' lives—they turned up for work that day but were sent away by the foreman who smelled whisky on their breath.

Mystery Visitor from Outer Space

A minor catastrophe was avoided in 1952 when the biggest-ever Alberta meteorite, weighing 107 kilograms, narrowly missed the town of Abee and fell into an adjacent field. Unlike most meteorites, the one that landed near Abee consisted of odd minerals in which oxygen is lacking and sulphur fills its place. Theories abound, but no one really knows where it came from, nor how it got there. The Abee meteorite is the largest-ever-found (in Canada) "enstatite chondrite," which is the rarest group of meteorites and has something to do with how the iron in the meteor melts on impact with the earth!

FROM DINOSAURS TO RALPH KLEIN

The following golden nuggets of information tell Alberta's story in a nutshell—the context of how the modern province came to be…

You Old Beast

The oldest inhabitants of ancient Alberta, dinosaurs, lived 75 million years ago.

Father of Fossils

Joseph Tyrrell first discovered fossils here in June 1884. He named the dino he unearthed *Albertosaurus sarcophagus* (close cousin of the *Tyrannosaurus rex*). The Royal Tyrrell Museum in Drumheller was named after him. The dinosaur was big and fast, 14 metres long and capable of reaching speeds of 60 kilometres per hour. Today, fossils are still easily found at Dinosaur Provincial Park, in the Red Deer Valley and at the Tyrrell Field Station, near the town of Brooks in southern Alberta.

The First People

Aboriginal people are thought to have come to America 20,000 to 30,000 years ago from Asia, crossing a land bridge that once joined with Alaska. That's why they call themselves First Nations—because they were the first people to settle the continent.

Ancient Albertans

The oldest "Albertans" are thought to have been from the Cree tribe, who lived near Vermilion Lakes about 12,000 years ago. The town of Vermilion was named 100 years ago for the red clay deposits in the surrounding lakes and river.

The First European

Anthony Henday became the first European to reach Alberta, near Innisfail, in 1754–55. A fur trader, he spent the winter with a group of Blackfeet. He traded and hunted bison with them and explored the vicinity of present-day Red Deer and Edmonton. Anthony Henday Drive, Edmonton's new highway, skirts the modern city and is part of the north–south trade corridor, linking Yellowhead Trail and Calgary Trail.

Alberta's First European Settlements

Fort Chipewyan was built by fur traders in 1778 near the mouth of the Athabasca River. Fort Edmonton was also built that same year.

David Thompson's Drive

In the 1790s, David Thompson began more than two decade's work of surveying Alberta for the North West Company and drawing the first good maps. The year 2007 marks the bicentennial anniversary of his discovery of a passage from the West through the Rockies to the Pacific Ocean. Drivers today can enjoy the David Thompson Highway, one of the most spectacular routes through the Rocky Mountains.

A Country Built on Beavers

By the 19th century, a wave of European beaver fur traders had arrived to find raw materials for posh toffs back home with a penchant for beaver top hats. But on the tail of these white men, a trail of destruction was left behind for the Natives.

Gun Laws Up to No Good

In the 18th century, millions of wild bison wandered through one-third of North America, from Canada to Mexico. But by 1905, guns controlled the prairies and bison had become almost extinct. The Plains tribes depended on the beasts for their own survival, so they too were also almost blown away.

Alberta's First Corporate Merger

In 1821, the North West Company merged with the Hudson's Bay Company—the great-great-grandfather of today's chain of The Bay department stores.

Alberta's First Missionary

Robert Rundle, a Methodist, arrived at Fort Edmonton in 1842. The first Roman Catholic missionary was Jean-Baptiste Thibault, who arrived at Lac Sainte Anne later the same year.

It Hardly Ever Rains on the Plains

In 1857, John Palliser's expedition deemed the prairies too dry for farming, thus delaying mass immigration for nearly half a century. Calgary's Palliser Hotel is named in John's honour.

Alberta's First Corporate Downsizing

In 1870, the Hudson's Bay Company turned the North-West Territories over to the newly formed Confederation of Canada, formed in 1867 between Ontario, Québec, Nova Scotia and New Brunswick.

Cops Put a Cork in It

In 1873, the Canadian government formed the North-West Mounted Police to maintain law and order because everyone was drinking too much. In 1874, the Mounties established their first post at Fort Macleod, primarily to stop the American whisky traders, who had established their own post, aptly nicknamed Fort Whoop-Up. The traders made massive profits selling hooch to the Natives, which eventually decimated their culture and their lives. High rates of fetal alcohol syndrome and alcohol addiction persist in Alberta today.

European Diseases and Alcohol Killed Aboriginals

Over the next few decades, the Native tribes were decimated by European afflictions and addictions. As the bison herds dwindled, First Nations peoples faced starvation and signed treaties to move onto reserve land, where the government pledged to feed them.

Modern Alberta is Born on the Rails

In 1883, the arrival of the railway made settlement of the West possible. The first sodbusters homesteaded about 16 kilometres north of Olds in 1885. The province's population boomed from 1000 non-Native settlers in 1881 to 17,500 10 years later.

The First Cowboys Come A-Calling

From 1888 onwards, ranchers arrived and thrived on the prairies, using the expertise of American cowboys like John Ware, who crossed the border from the U.S. in 1876, bringing with him the province's first herd of cattle. Thus were born Alberta's cattle and meat-packing businesses, two of today's most important industries.

Stellar Stettler

The town's growth was spectacular—its first building was constructed in 1890, but just one year later there were 70 businesses, two doctors, a dentist, a lawyer, two pharmacists and two banks in the village.

Gold Diggers Fortune-ate or Fatal

In 1896, once gold was discovered in the Klondike region of the Yukon, 100,000 fortune seekers arrived within six months. Many travelled through Edmonton, which was the last port of call before the long trek north. The city grew exponentially. It was also the last civilized place many of the prospectors would ever see, because 70,000 died on the journey.

Immigrants Wanted

Farming really took off in 1897, when Canada's minister of the interior, Clifford Sifton, launched a massive advertising campaign to convince European homesteaders to settle the prairies.

Population Explosion

The result of Sifton's campaign was spectacular. Alberta's population grew to 73,000 in 1901; to 374,000 in 1911; and to 584,000 in 1921! Multiculturalism was born, with homesteaders coming predominantly from Ontario, Britain, the United States, Germany, the Ukraine and Romania.

Settling Down

The earliest settlements congregated into towns near convenient railway access and then spread slowly to other parts of the province. By 1904, the fastest growing community in Canada was Red Deer.

Cheap Digs

In 1905, a homestead entry cost $10 for a 64-hectare piece of land. Title to the property was granted to any man over the age of 21 after three years on condition that the settlers built a house on their property, they cultivated at least 16 hectares of land, and they lived on the land at least six months out of each of their first three years in Canada.

DID YOU KNOW?

Early settlers to the province paid a mere $10 a pop for a chunk of land at the turn of the 20th century. Things have changed a lot since then. An average home in Edmonton in 2004 would have set you back $167,000, the lowest of any major Canadian city. The same real estate in Calgary has a $212,000 price tag, $297,000 in Toronto and a whopping $345,000 in Vancouver.

The Province Graduates to Higher Education

The province's first post-secondary institution was the University of Alberta, established in 1907. The University of Calgary was established in 1965.

The First Alberta Strike

In 1908, "Old Glory" in the Bow Island gas field was Alberta's first well and the first major discovery in commercial oil and gas exploration. Developing the field led to the first pipelines delivering natural gas to Alberta communities.

Ladies Wanted

In 1911, most Albertans were men. In places like Calgary, guys outnumbered gals by 155 to 100. To redress the balance, requests were sent for "gentlewomen" to emigrate through the British Women's Emigration Association, which had been established in 1862 to rectify the overabundance of single women in the UK.

Ladies Working

It worked out well, because today a quarter of all farm operators in Alberta are women. Furthermore, 33% of those whose primary source of income comes from agriculture in Alberta are women.

DID YOU  KNOW?

Today there's a tiny surplus of males over females in the province up to age 55, and then the tables turn and there are more older women alive than there are men.

 In 1909, by the end of its first year in operation, the United Farmers of Alberta (UFA) boasted 5000 member farmers. By 1921, the organization had become a political force in Alberta by winning 38 of the 44 seats in the Legislature. The UFA's most significant accomplishment was Premier John Brownlee's 1929 transfer of oil and mineral rights to the province, a move that contributes to the $8.8 billion provincial surplus that Alberta residents enjoyed in 2005.

The Cost of World War I

Of the 39,000 Albertans who served in the war, 6000 lost their lives.

First Explosion
In 1914, oil was discovered in the Turner Valley, kicking off Alberta's fist oil boom.

Women Can Vote

The big year for the ladies came in 1916.

Down and Very Nearly Out

Alberta suffered severely during the Great Depression of the early 1930s. Drought, grasshopper plagues and soil erosion drove many farmers off their land. Then the price of wheat fell. Consequently, many farmers went bankrupt—10,000 farms closed in the five years from 1931 onwards.

DID YOU  KNOW?

Canada's largest prisoner-of-war camps during World War II were in Medicine Hat and Lethbridge. The 12,000 German prisoners held in Lethbridge equalled the city's population at the time.

Second Time Around

In World War II, 77,704 Albertans enlisted, and 3350 died in combat.

War Bonanza

World War II lifted Alberta out of the Depression with manufacturing, oil and the first big push to encourage the beef industry.

Farmers Out, Credit In

In 1935, the United Farmers Association government lost the vote to the Social Credit Party.

 Imperial Oil's 1947 landmark crude oil discovery at Leduc, 40 kilometres southwest of Edmonton, marked the beginning of the modern oil industry in Canada. By 1938, Alberta had 294 producing wells, and by 1953, there were 4272. Revenue from oil went up 40-fold from 1945 to 1955.

Unfit for Farming

The proportion of the population living on farms went down from 41% in 1946 to 19% by 1966.

Boom, Boom, Another Oil Boom
Oil boomed again in 1961, and the provincial population nearly doubled from the previous 15 years.

First to Vote at Last
Alberta granted First Nations peoples the right to vote in 1965. Québec remained the only other province left to do so.

Tories In and Not Budging

The Progressive Conservatives won control of the provincial government in 1971, and they haven't left since.

City of Champions

In 1984, the Edmonton Oilers won the first of five Stanley Cups.

The Big Bust
In the 1980s, oil prices collapsed—and so did Alberta's economy. By 1986, oil had hit its lowest-ever price per barrel of $10. Sixty-five thousand people lost their jobs, and food banks became prevalent. The province experienced its worst economic crisis since the Depression.

Prices Up, Up and Away

During the 1980s crisis, inflation rates in the whole of Canada soared so high that the lowest rate nationally was Calgary's at a staggering 36.8%. Edmonton tied for second lowest at 38.1%, but inflation in Toronto was a crippling 52.8%.

Diversify or Die

In the 1990s, the government encouraged forestry as the major industry alternative to oil in case of another bust.

DID YOU  KNOW?

In 2000, in Alberta, a woman's life expectancy at birth was 81.9 years, whereas a man's was a mere 77.1 years.

No More Debt

Ralph Klein was elected premier in 1993, promising to eliminate budget deficits—a goal that took five years to achieve—and to cut debt, which took until 2004.

BY THE NUMBERS

Alberta Gets Bigger

Alberta is Canada's fourth-largest province by population.
The population growth since the turn of the century goes
like this:

1900	73,000 total population
1941	769,169 total population
1971	1,600,000 total population
2004	3,200,000 total population

SPREAD AROUND THE PROVINCE

In 2004, Albertans lived in:

Calgary	933,493 (*)
Edmonton	707,271 (^)
Red Deer	75,923
Strathcona County	75,949 (^)
Lethbridge	72,717
Regional Municipality of Wood Buffalo	67,105
St. Albert	54,588 (^)
Medicine Hat	51,249
Grande Prairie	40,226
Municipality of Rocky View	30,418 (*)

(*) part of the greater Calgary area
(^) part of the greater Edmonton area

DID YOU  KNOW?

About 5.5 million cattle can be found in Alberta, outnumbering people by almost 2 to 1.

Move Over

From 1999 to 2004, Alberta's population has grown the fastest of all the provinces, at a rate of 1.4%. In 2001, 16,290 people settled here—6000 were newcomers to Canada, while the rest were from other parts of the country.

Foreigners are Few
Fifteen percent of Alberta's population was foreign-born in 2001, the third highest concentration in Canada. In 2001, the two provinces with the highest proportion of people born outside the country, at a rate of around 30%, were Ontario and British Columbia.

Canadians Love Alberta

Alberta has the highest number of Canadians moving in, compared to those moving out. From July 2003 to June 2004, 10,902 Canadians came to Alberta from other provinces. The only other provinces to have more Canadians coming than leaving were British Columbia and Prince Edward Island, at 7333 and 299 respectively.

DID YOU KNOW?

Alberta has the youngest population of all the provinces—58% of Albertans are under the age of 40. In Manitoba, Saskatchewan and Ontario, 55% of the population is over 40. Nova Scotia has the oldest average population, with 14% over the age of 65.

The Youngest of the Young
At 30 years, Fort McMurray has the lowest average age of any Alberta community. Less than 2000 of the city's 60,983 residents are over 60 years of age. Because most of the town's inhabitants work the oil patch, 10% more men than women live there.

THE VERY FIRST ALBERTANS

Alberta is home to 43 First Nations groups and 114 reserves.

The Beaver

The Beaver First Nation is located near High Level, in northern Alberta. They originally existed in small nomadic family groups and numbered about 1000. The Beaver were decimated by European diseases and were the last band to sign Treaty 8 in 1900.

BlackFoot (Siksika)

Today, about 4200 people live on the Siksika Nation, which is about an hour's drive east of Calgary.

A CONFEDERATION OF TRIBES

The Blackfoot people are part of the Blackfoot Confederacy, a collective term for the tribes that live throughout the prairies of western Canada, which includes the Peigan and the Blood tribes. The Confederacy signed Treaty 7 in 1877. Since then, the Siksika have managed to overcome the harsh realities of the reserves and survive through agriculture.

POWERFUL ON THE PRAIRIES

At the height of their power, the Blackfoot commanded territory from the North Saskatchewan River, south to the Missouri River. The first to trade with the settlers, the Blackfoot prospered for a while, until the whisky trade wiped many out.

GOING IT ALONE

The Blackfoot Nation is now actively seeking self-government and impunity from the jurisdiction of the 1867 Indian Act.

BLOOD OR KAINAI

The Kainai tribe is the largest in southern Alberta to sign a treaty, Treaty 7. Today's Kainaiwa reserve is near Lethbridge, where the community has built all its own infrastucture. Cash is generated through farming, artisan activities, irrigation projects, cattle operations, trades and environmental preservation projects.

PEIGAN OR PIIKANI—THE SMALLEST AND THE LARGEST TRIBE

This group is made up of the North Peigan and South Peigan. The North Peigan are Canadian and are the smallest clan of the Blackfoot Confederacy to have signed a treaty, number 7. But grouped with their southern counterparts, who live in Montana, the Peigan together make up the largest tribe within the Confederacy. The Peigan were the first Nation to demand a vote in provincial elections and the first to take over administration of their own reserve.

CREE

The Cree Nation is made up of both the Plains Cree and the Woodland Cree, which is the largest aboriginal group in northern Alberta.

FIRST IN FUR TRADE

The Woodland Cree Nation was also one of the first to trade with European fur traders, as early as the 1600s. The Cree now live in Treaty 8 reserves near Lesser Slave Lake in north-western Alberta.

Dené—the Most Northerly Tribe in Alberta

Historically the Dené lived on fish and caribou. They had no leaders and developed a reputation for being peaceful and having a rich storytelling tradition. The northernmost Dené tribe signed Treaty 8 in 1900, but the southern Dené signed Treaty 11 much later in 1921, and their reserves are in the High Level area. The population today numbers just over 4000. Until recently, family life was often disrupted when the young left for school and work, but newer jobs in the oil and forestry industries are allowing tribe members to stay and live with their families.

Métis' Mixed Fortunes

The Métis (meaning "mixed") are unique in their development. Most are descendants of the earliest French and English fur traders and predominantly Cree women who lived in central and southern Alberta.

NO TREATY BENEFITS

The Métis were never covered by any of the treaties and therefore never received any of the benefits. By the 1920s, they had become the poorest of the poor.

A NATION RECOGNIZED

Only in 1938, with the passing of the Métis Betterment Act, did the Alberta government allocate land for the Métis, which has resulted in today's communities at Bison Lake, East Prairie, Elizabeth, Fishing Lake, Gift Lake, Kikino, Paddle Prairie and Peavine.

The Stoney Hunters

The people of the Stoney Nation, also known as the Assiniboine, were nomadic hunters of the Sioux Nation. The Stoney was one of the few tribes to listen to the missionaries and many converted to the Methodist faith in the 1800s. The leaders signed Treaties 6 and 7 in the 1870s.

THE FIRST NATION TO REKINDLE ITS OWN CULTURE

The Stoney Nation became one of the first to create its own cultural program, encouraging the teaching of the Stoney language, introducing university courses about its culture and creating a wilderness program to preserve the environment.

OTHER EARLY ALBERTANS

More Germans than Anyone Else

After the British and French ethnic groups, there are more people of German ancestry in Alberta than any other. The same goes for the rest of Canada, actually. Most came to Alberta from the U.S. once the Edmonton Railway opened in 1892. Many were suspected of being loyal to Germany during the war years and were locked up in internment camps. Those who came after the two world wars integrated *über* quickly and successfully into the province.

Lots of Scots

Scots are the largest single group of English-speaking origin in Alberta, and there isn't any area of public life they haven't excelled in. Scots were among the first settlers, including prominent members of the North-West Mounted Police, such as Colonel James Macleod, who founded the fort of the same name south of Calgary. Alexander Rutherford, an Ontario-born Scot, became the province's first premier in 1905.

The Luck o' the Irish

Those from the Emerald Isle make up the second biggest English-speaking group in Alberta. They publish their own paper, *The Edmonton Blarney*, and are most visible on Saint Patrick's Day, which is celebrated by both Irish and non-Irish Canadians alike.

Just Like Home for Ukrainians

In 2001, almost 10% of Albertans could trace their heritage to the Ukraine. Undeterred by Albertan winters, which were just as severe as their own, Ivan Pylypow and Wasyl Eleniak were the first officially documented Ukrainian homesteaders to settle in Alberta, about 80 kilometres northeast of Edmonton in 1891. So many other Ukrainian immigrants soon followed that the area became the largest settlement of its kind in Canada, although Lethbridge, Drumheller and Calgary also had sizeable communities.

Chinese Construct Railways and Towns

Without the Chinese labourers in the late 1880s, Alberta's railways would never have been built. But the entry or "head" tax, first imposed in 1885, was raised from $100 to $500 in 1903, which made it almost impossible for these men to bring wives and children to Canada, ensuring that the Chinese population remained predominantly male for a long time.

DID YOU KNOW?

It wasn't until the late 1960s that Chinese people were welcomed into Canada, and today they comprise the largest proportion of the visible minority population in the country. British Columbia has the highest population of all at 44% of the visible minority, and Alberta comes in second with 30%. Today, most Chinese settle in urban areas, and there's a thriving Chinatown in every major Alberta city—the biggest is in Calgary.

Norman Kwong, the Lieutenant-Governor of Alberta, appointed in 2005, was the first Chinese Canadian to play in the Canadian Football League. He earned the nickname the "China Clipper" when he played for the Edmonton Eskimos. He won four Grey Cups as a player and was co-owner of the Calgary Stampeders when they won their first Grey Cup in 1989. He is an inductee of the CFL Alberta and Canadian Halls of Fame.

Indian Melting Pot

"East Indians" is the collective Canadian term given to all those who come from the Indian subcontinent, but to lump them all together is like saying all Europeans speak, eat and believe the same stuff. People from India, Pakistan, Sri Lanka, Bhutan, Nepal and Afghanistan brought to Alberta languages and religions so diverse that they are often completely unintelligible to the other groups of so-called "Indians." Their religions are equally diverse and include Hindu, Sikh, Muslim, Parsi, Christian, Sufi and Baha'i, to name but a few. But however different their cultures, Canadian immigration policy initially treated them all the same.

DID YOU **KNOW?**

East Indians settled in Canada relatively late because of a law stating that immigrants had to come *directly* from their country of origin. You'd have had to have been Superman to get to Canada from India in 1907 without going through another country. The "continuous passage" legislation wasn't lifted until 1948, and the 1960s saw a massive influx of people from India, most of whom were well educated and quickly integrated into the province's multi-ethnic mosaic.

Canada's First Mosque

The Al Rashid Mosque was built in Edmonton in 1937 by the Lebanese community.

Few Jews

Two brothers, Jacob and William Diamond, were among the first Jewish people to settle in Alberta, in 1888 and 1892 respectively. Of today's 350,000 Canadian Jews, only about 13,000 live in Alberta, 7000 of those in Calgary. Early immigration of Jewish settlers was hindered by pro-Christian Social Credit Party policies, and the Jewish preference for settling in urban rather than rural areas flew in the face of the government's aims to expand agriculture.

PANORAMIC PRAIRIES BUT FEW FOLK

One of the best things about Alberta is its wondrous skies, and with so few people living here, skyscrapers don't block the view. That's because the province's population density sits near the bottom of the world rankings—Alberta takes 184th place out of 193. To be fair, most of the rest of Canada, except those condensed into PEI and Nova Scotia, also rank near the 184th position. (By the way, population density is measured by the number of people divided by size of the area in which they live.)

Sixth-Densest Population in Canada

Alberta is the sixth most densely populated region out of all Canadian provinces and territories, with 4.65 people/km^2. (Aah, statistics. So what's happened to the remaining 0.35 of that person, huh?)

DID YOU KNOW?

Greenland is the country with the lowest population density in the world—only 0.03 people/km^2, the same population density as (surprise, surprise) the three coldest territories in Canada, which have an equally tiny number of people hardy enough to live there.

Here's how population density in the provinces and territories compare to each other and to other countries.

POPULATION DENSITY OF CANADIAN PROVINCES AND TERRITORIES AND SELECTED COUNTRIES WORLDWIDE

WORLD RANKING 1–193	CANADIAN RANKING 1–13	CANADIAN PROVINCE OR TERRITORY OR OTHER COUNTRY	PEOPLE PER SQUARE KILOMETRE
1		Monaco	16,620.00
2		Singapore	6389.00
19		India	329.00
33		United Kingdom	243.00
54		People's Republic of China	136.00
92		Ukraine	79.00
127		**World Average**	42.00
143		United States	30.00
149	1	PEI	23.80
160	2	Nova Scotia	17.16
169	3	Ontario	12.57
174	4	New Brunswick	10.22
183	5	Québec	5.33
183	6	**Alberta**	4.65
184	7	British Colombia	4.22
191		**Canada**	3.33
193	8	Manitoba	2.03
193	9	Saskatchewan	1.67
193	10	Newfoundland	1.38
193	11	Nanavut	0.06
193	12	Yukon	0.06
193	13	Northwest Territories	0.03

COWBOYS

Since there are so many people swaggering around Alberta wearing white Stetsons and cowboy boots, here's a nod to their heritage in a quick data roundup.

One Law for the Cowboys...

Leftover from the early cowboy era, some Alberta laws have never been repealed. So, technically...

> "If you are released from prison, it is required that you are given a handgun with bullets and a horse, so you can ride out of town."

And

> "Businesses must provide rails for tying up horses."

In Celebration of our Bovine Buddies
- More than 100 medicines used by humans come from cattle.
- One cowhide can produce enough leather to make 20 footballs, 18 soccer balls, 18 volleyballs or 12 basketballs.
- The average cow makes more than 40,000 jaw movements per day.
- It is possible to lead a cow upstairs but not downstairs, because a cow's knees can't bend properly to walk back down.

 The Calgary Stampede started in 1912 and was billed then, as it still is today, as "The Greatest Outdoor Show on Earth."

Loads of Money
The first Calgary Stampede was the richest rodeo competition in North America at the time, with prize money totalling $20,000. And today's Greatest Outdoor Show on Earth is also a great way to make cash—$1 million in prize money and $125 million pumped into the Calgary economy from visitors.

 A sign in Wetaskiwin in 1917 read: "It is against the law to tie a male horse next to a female horse on Main Street."

Saddle 'em Up and Ride 'em Out

One of the first cowboys to arrive in Alberta was John Ware, who was born a black slave but made Calgary his home in 1882 after the American Civil War. John became a legendary bronco rider and brilliant teacher of cowboy skills. He was instrumental in the success of Alberta's most successful ranch, the Bar U, which made millions from 1882 to 1950 and is a cowboy museum today.

 Morris "Two-Gun" Cohen was a pistol-carrying Calgary gambler and adventurer who became a bodyguard for Chinese revolutionary leader Sun Yat-sen in 1922.

Get Off Your Horse and Feed Your Cow

From 1902 to 1945, cattle were rounded up and held in herds so they could be fed on hay or grain that had been purposefully grown and stored. Feeding them had to become mechanized. Canada's first abattoirs were built next to Alberta railway stations for easy transport, and meat-packing plants materialized—thus was born today's modern cattle processing industry.

Wheat is Greener than Grass

By 1923, wheat grown to feed people and cattle made Canada the number one producer of grain in the world.

Very Concentrated Feeding

After World War II, cattle were fed in modern mechanized feedlots. By the mid-1980s, 10% of Alberta's feedlots fed 40% of the province's cattle.

Grassroots at the Bottom

Today's cattle industry is about lots of little guys at the bottom and a few big rich guys at the top.

- ☛ **A little goes a long way.** Calf/cow producers use the latest scientific techniques available to breed and raise a better cow. Typically, there are a large number of producers making small numbers of calves, around 100 each.
- ☛ **Feedlot operators.** There are a few medium-large companies each feeding a lot of cows.
- ☛ **Meat packers.** Alberta beef is processed by just three "king companies": Cargill, Lakeside and XL Foods. Their profits *rose* 281% during the mad-cow crisis, from $79 per cow to $216.52 a head.

The Cowboy Trail

If you played cowboys and Indians as a kid, you can do it for real as a grown up today, but it will take you days to drive the 640-kilometre-long Cowboy Trail and take in all the sites. The route starts at Mayerthorpe (northwest of Edmonton) and goes south, finally ending in Cardston, just a lasso's throw away from Montana. Along the way, you can ride a horse along beautiful Bragg Creek, take in the Stampede in Calgary, discover Turner Valley where oil was first discovered, visit the Bar U Ranch at Longview, as well as Kootenai Brown's Pioneer Village, Head-Smashed-In Buffalo Jump, Waterton Lakes National Park and then head east to Cardston, where the Remington-Alberta Carriage Centre houses wagons from the Wild West.

DID YOU KNOW?

The same dirt has been used to cover Edmonton's Rexall Place for the Canadian Finals Rodeo for 30 years. It's cleaned up and returned every year. The soil has to have just the right composition, so it's not too hard to fall on or too soft to slip in.

The Calgary Stampede is Canada's Largest Annual Event

Top attractions include one of the world's biggest rodeo competitions, stage shows, concerts, agricultural competitions and really-dangerous-but-thrilling chuckwagon races. In 2005, attendance of 1,242,928 broke all previous records.

DID YOU  KNOW?

Visitors to Calgary Stampede breakfasts consume more than 4536 kilograms of pancake batter, 1814 kilograms of bacon and sausage, 5000 bottles of syrup and 85,000 containers of juice.

How Good a Stampeder are You?

1) Who changed his or her name to "Linder One Spot" in order to enter a race and why?
2) How large is Stampede Park?
   a) 100 hectares
   b) 55.4 hectares
   c) 5.5 hectares
3) What race is featured on a 1975 Canadian postage stamp?
4) How many contestants compete in the rodeo?
5) How many volunteers does it take to service the Stampede?
   a) 18,000
   b) 1800
   c) 3010

5) b) 1800
4) 500
3) The Wild Horse Race
2) c) 55.4 hectares (137 acres)
her identity was discovered.
Event by entering as Linder One Spot. She made three rides before
1) In 1952, Linda One Spot broke into the Boys Wild Steer Riding

ALBERTA'S ANIMALS

Grrrrrizzly

Only one person has been killed by a grizzly in Alberta in the last 50 years. In June 2005, a jogger, Isabelle Dubé, 36, was attacked and mauled to death by a bear that rangers had tried to relocate away from Canmore, but the bear came back and found the runner on a path.

Photo Opportunity

A few tourists have been crazy enough to take big risks for a snap that might have gotten their necks snapped. One set of idiotic parents, in 2004, put honey on their two-year-old's face...so they could take a photo of the bear licking it off. In 2002, a bear charged a big group of tourists out on a hike, because they had surrounded him, also in the hope of getting its picture.

DID YOU KNOW?

Alberta is home to 20,000 of Canada's total elk population of 70,000. Many of them live in Elk Island National Park, east of Edmonton.

Bison Back from the Dead

There have been two attempts to save Alberta's bison from extinction. Wood Buffalo National Park was created in 1922 to preserve the last remaining herd of wild wood bison. It covers 45,000 km² of Alberta and the Northwest Territories. A disease hit the herd a decade later, and the bison were nearly wiped out once again. But in 1957, a tiny herd of 200 was discovered and moved to Elk Island National Park for safekeeping in case disease hits the Wood Buffalo herd again. There are 3500 bison at Wood Buffalo and 350 at Elk Island.

Endangered in Alberta

Alberta's endangered species list includes the swift fox, Ord's kangaroo rat (which *is* a rodent, but not technically a rat or a kangaroo), sage grouse, piping plover, whooping crane, wood bison and American white pelican.

Threatened in Alberta

The woodland and barren ground caribou, ferruginous hawk, burrowing owl, peregrine falcon, trumpeter swan and northern leopard frog are on Alberta's list of threatened species.

Official Concern

The bull trout, the province's official fish, is a "species of special concern." A species is of special concern when it is particularly sensitive to human activities or vulnerable to natural events.

Alberta's Cats

Lynx and bobcats are found in Alberta. Cougars are, too, but they are so wary of humans that their numbers are extremely tough to measure. Twenty are believed to roam around Banff National Park and, for the first time since records began in 1906, a cougar was sighted at Elk Island National Park in 2003.

TRAINS...

Past and Present Travel Times from Edmonton to Calgary

- ☛ Pre-1891: Three treacherous, bandit-ridden days by stagecoach. (Even longer by wagon, which is how most of the homesteaders arrived.)
- ☛ Post-1891: Twelve hours by train.
- ☛ Today the distance can be driven in less than three hours (legally).

The West's First Railroad Made Tracks in 1883

That was the date when the Canadian Pacific Railway (CPR) established a line from eastern Canada through Medicine Hat and Calgary to Banff.

DID YOU  KNOW?

The Calgary–Edmonton line was built in 1890, but trains east of Edmonton to Winnipeg didn't go full steam ahead until 1905.

From Station to Namesake

The Canadian National (CN) railway claims responsibility for creating 500 communities in the Prairie Provinces. Many towns still bear the names of eminent railway workers who helped establish them.

 The first shack went up in Olds in 1890 next to a railway siding, and by 1904, the hamlet around the railway station boasted a population of 100. It was named after the first CPR station master, George Olds. Olds was also the first town to be incorporated in the new Province of Alberta in 1905.

Edmonton's First Station

The city's first train station was built at 105th Avenue and 113th Street, and it became the centre of Edmonton's warehouse district, where the Baccarat Casino stands today. At the time it was built, the station marked the northern extremity of the city.

On and Off the Rails

Strathcona's first station, built in 1909, was sold in 1956, demolished and then rebuilt in the style of the old station. Today it is the Iron Horse Pub, where a lot of young folk go off the rails on Friday and Saturday nights.

What Goes Up Must Come Down

If not for the trains, there wouldn't have been any wooden grain elevators. They sprang up every 10 kilometres of track, to store and ease the loading of grain from surrounding farms directly into trains for transportation across the country and across the globe. Today there are just a handful left as tourist attractions—most have been replaced with concrete mega-elevators, usually found outside town limits.

Little Light Trains get Bigger

Edmonton's LRT system has a total of 11 stations, five above ground. Future expansion plans, with a budget of $595 million, will add approximately 7.5 kilometres to the city's LRT line and two new stations.

Edmonton was the first city in North America to have a light rail railway…and the old one still operates as a tourist attraction from May through October.

C-Train

The C-train, Calgary's light-rail train system, runs on 41.2 kilometres of track. Unique to the system is that its power is completely wind generated and is thus completely free of emissions.

Express in the West

The West's equivalent of the luxurious Orient Express is the luxury two-day train ride from Edmonton to Vancouver through the Rockies. The price is mountainous, too.

PLANES...

Planes on the Plains

On the wings of WWII came army and air force bases in Cold Lake and Wainwright, which still exist today. Along with a dozen flight training schools, Edmonton's airports collectively became the busiest in Canada with an average of 800 inbound flights a day.

Canada's first licensed municipal airport was Edmonton's Blatchford Field, which opened in 1927.

DID YOU KNOW?

There is an international airport in each of the province's two major cities, Calgary and Edmonton, third and fifth busiest in Canada respectively. There are also 20 provincial airports.

Flying So High, So Young

The youngest pilot to fly across Canada was nine-year-old Emma Houlston of Medicine Hat in 1988, who flew to St. John's, Newfoundland, in 13 stages. Seven-year-old Joanna Mullen of Edmonton is Canada's youngest pilot. She got her license on her seventh birthday.

AND AUTOMOBILES...

For Whom the Bell Tolls

The most likely time to have a fatal car accident in Alberta is on a Sunday between 3:00 and 7:00 PM. The most likely day is Heritage Day.

DID YOU KNOW?

A motor vehicle collision occurs once every 72 seconds in Alberta.

Don't Fence Me In

The province's rural drivers are more likely to break the law by not wearing a seatbelt than urban drivers—76% of country folk go without a belt, but 84% of city dwellers do buckle up.

Drunk at the Wheel

In 2003, Edmonton and Calgary had higher rates of impaired drivers than anywhere else in Canada. Of all provinces, Alberta ranks second worst for drunk driving. Saskatchewan wins the booby prize for being the worst.

DID YOU KNOW?

An average of 400 people a year die on Alberta's roads. One-third of these deaths is caused by drunk drivers—one of the highest rates in the country.

And Throw Away the Key

In Prince Edward Island,-91% of those found guilty of impaired driving landed in prison, compared with-28% in Newfoundland and Labrador, 10% in Alberta and-4% in Nova Scotia.

Alberta is graced with 168,014 kilometres of highways and roads, though only 31,000 kilometres are paved.

First Fast Formula

Alberta's first grand prix was held at the City Centre Airport in Edmonton in 2005. French driver Sébastien Bourdais won the inaugural race. More than 200,000 people attended the three-day event, including veteran actor Paul Newman.

Albertans Keep on Trucking

In 2004, new motor vehicle sales declined in all provinces except Alberta and British Columbia.

MUST-SEE PLACES IN THE PROVINCE

Worth Preserving

Alberta is home to 40% of Canada's United Nations World Heritage Sites, areas designated by UNESCO. Of the 13 national sites, Alberta's five are:

☛ Dinosaur Provincial Park—The world's most extensive display of dinosaur specimens

☛ Head-Smashed-In Buffalo Jump—The best-preserved bison jump site in the world

☛ Wood Buffalo National Park—Home to the world's largest herd of free-roaming bison

☛ The Canadian Rocky Mountain Parks—Banff (Canada's oldest) and Jasper (Canada's largest mountain park)

☛ Waterton Glacier International Peace Park—The world's first peace park

DID YOU KNOW?

Alberta has more than 530 parks (including five national and 300 provincial), 600 lakes and 245 rivers and protected areas. You can find everything from beaches (not bad considering it's a 12-hour drive to the sea) to remote backcountry adventure playgrounds. The province has more than 275 golf courses and six mountain ski resorts, as well as 66 regional ski hills.

Too Many Tourists?

Over 8 million visitors visit Alberta's provincial parks and recreation areas annually. But it's not much fun to cruise Banff's high street in high summer when the number of daily visitors can average 50,000.

Tourism is Alberta's sixth largest industry and employs 100,000 people, generating $4.6 billion in revenues in 2004.

Twenty-two million visitors came to Alberta for the 1988 Winter Olympics. It was the first Olympics to make a profit.

Rocky Mountain High

The highest mountain in Alberta is Mt. Columbia at 3747 metres (12,294 feet).

All-Time Low

The lowest point in Alberta is where the Salt River enters the Northwest Territories: 183 metres (600 feet).

Lovely Lakes

The world's second largest glacier-fed lake is Maligne Lake in Jasper National Park. But Moraine Lake in Banff National Park is one of the world's most photographed lakes. It used to appear on the old $20 bill.

Canada's national park system started in 1887 when 673 km² of land surrounding the hot springs at Banff were set aside. It was called "Rocky Mountains Park" and was Canada's first national park. Today, Banff National Park spans 6641 km² and is jam-packed with some of the most stunning scenery anywhere in the world—valleys, mountains, glaciers, forests, meadows, rivers, lakes. Mmmmm.

DID YOU  KNOW?

The highest restaurant in Canada is the Panoramic Summit Restaurant found at the top of Banff's Sulphur Mountain.

Canada's Longest Gondola Ride

Up, up and away go the skiers to get to the pistes at Sunshine Village in Banff National Park.

 Jasper National Park has a 1000-kilometre network of hiking trails and one of the most extensive backcountry trail systems in the world.

Jasper's Peak
The park's most famous and tallest mountain is the 3363-metre-high Mount Edith Cavell.

Mountainous Pampering
The most luxurious and expensive place to stay is the Jasper Park Lodge.

Easy on the Ice

The Columbia Icefields is one of the most accessible glacier fields in the world and one of the biggest concentrations of snow and ice south of the Arctic Circle. The field covers an area of 325 km² (contained within both Banff and Jasper National Parks), and in some places the ice forms sheets 365 metres thick.

They're Big, They're Bad and They're Anything but Ugly
Badlands are formed when glaciers melt and the runoff carves massive gorges in the countryside, digging deep wherever the ground beneath is soft. The biggest stretch in Alberta is 300 kilometres of beautiful multi-layered rock formations found in Dinosaur Provincial Park. The terrain looks like "outer space meets the desert."

Ten kilometres west of Okotoks is one of the largest "erratics" in North America—18,000 tonnes of rock. An erratic is a lump of rock that is taken from the site of its original formation by a glacier and dumped somewhere when the ice melts. Big Rock is thought to be an outcrop of Mount Edith Cavell, hundreds of kilometres away.

Howdy Hoodoo

First Nations peoples thought the strange rock formations known as "hoodoos" actually housed the spirits of ancestors. Their odd shapes are the result of erosion over millions of years, which leaves behind harder rock in bizarre wind-and-rain-weathered formations. Alberta boasts three areas where you can find these wonderful natural oddities: near Banff, east of Drumheller and 65 kilometres northeast of Hinton.

EVERY TOWN TELLS A STORY

Here's a list of remarkable tidbits about the province's towns.

BONNYVILLE
Alberta has the largest Francophone population of all the western provinces, with Bonnyville claiming a large percentage.

BROOKS
This town is a mini "United Nations," with more than 100 distinct languages spoken among a population of just 11,600, making it one of the most multicultural towns in the province. Brooks is home to Lakeside Farm Industries Ltd.— one of Canada's biggest slaughterhouses—which processes up to 4000 cattle a day.

CARDSTON
Located 25 kilometres north of the U.S. border with Montana, this town is home to the biggest Mormon Temple in Canada. It looks like a Mayan or Aztec temple and was completed in 1923. There are no liquor stores in the town, and the advertising of tobacco products is also banned in a bylaw.

CAMROSE
This agricultural community hosts the largest outdoor country and western festival in Canada, the Big Valley Jamboree—no confusion, there's no valley in sight.

COLD LAKE
Located in northeastern Alberta, its claim to fame is CFB Cold Lake—the largest airforce base in Canada. The town also has a lake, Alberta's seventh largest, that is (yep) very cold

except for the first few metres on the surface. It sinks to a depth of 111 metres, is one of province's deepest and clearest bodies of water, and is home to the greatest number of fish species of any lake in Alberta. A 250-boat marina on the lake is one of the largest inland marinas in Canada.

CYPRESS HILLS
This region is the only spot in the whole province untouched by the glaciers during the last ice age. As a result, unique ecosystems are found there, as well as shreds of evidence that humans lived in the area 7000 years ago.

FORT MACLEOD
This historic town is home to the Fort Museum, which celebrates North-West Mounted Police history. The fort features the restoration of the barracks as they were in 1884, and the Main Street Restoration Project includes 60 buildings that provide a cross-section of Alberta history.

FALHER
Located in the Smokey River Region of Alberta's Peace District, you'll find the Honey Capital of Canada. This town produces 4.5 million kilograms of honey annually.

GRIMSHAW
The Mackenzie Highway starts at this town and is the only very vital route north of 60 all the way to Yellowknife. Until recently, of its 690 kilometres of road, only the first 180 kilometres were paved, so the journey used to be a gruelling one on gravel. Most of it today is a paved two-lane highway.

HIGH RIVER
Famous as the setting for author W.O Mitchell's classic stories, *Jake and the Kid*, it is also the home of former Prime Minister Joe Clark and the burial place of Calgary Stampede founder Guy Weadick.

HINTON

Apart from being the last town you hit before reaching the Rocky Mountains on the drive west from Edmonton, the town's other claim to fame is that its location has moved 10 times along a 12-kilometre length of railway line in the last 100 years.

HIGH PRAIRIE

Home first of all to the Beaver Nation, today, apart from spectacular scenery, it is home to the Golden Walleye Classic, Canada's richest and North America's largest fishing tournament.

INDIAN CABINS

Just 200 metres off the Old Mackenzie Highway near the town of Indian Cabins is the site of one of the few remaining First Nations tree graves. Seventy years ago an infant was buried in a hollowed log, which was nailed shut and hung between two tree limbs.

LAKE LOUISE
This outdoor-recreation mecca is the highest town in Canada at 1540 metres.

LAC LA BICHE
One of Alberta's oldest communities, dating back to David Thompson's visit in 1798, is the site where Alberta's first wheat was grown. The surrounding area has 150 lakes, 1200 campsites and Alberta's only backcountry canoe circuit, where you can paddle through several interconnected lakes and even portage your belongings just like them ol' pioneers.

LEESHORE
This town holds the Alberta record for the first-ever sighting of a crop circle. There have been 34 since then.

LETHBRIDGE
Having started life as the whisky trader's post Fort Whoop-Up, it prospered with the discovery of the Oldman coal mine nearby. There's a Whoop-Up Days festival every August. Lethbridge is Alberta's fourth largest city by population, third largest in area.

LONGVIEW
With five high-class restaurants in a town of only 300 residents, Longview likes to think of itself as "the town that tastes like New York."

McLENNAN
Located on the shores of Kimiwan Lake, McLennan is known as the "Bird Capital of Canada." It is estimated that from 15,000 to 20,000 shorebirds flock here annually, as well as 200,000 waterfowl and land birds.

PONOKA
This farm town hosts Canada's largest single-day livestock auction as well as the Ponoka Stampede.

RED DEER

St. Mary's Church, designed by Douglas Cardinal, a Métis brought up in the residential school system, is one of the most stunning pieces of modern architecture in the province. The building is round and made of red brick to blend in with the countryside. Today, students of architecture in Canada examine its construction and appeal, even though when it was first built, many were outraged by the church's fortress-like design.

SWAN HILLS

This town is the site of the third largest oilfield in Canada, which produces nearly one-third of Alberta's oil, drilled by four major companies. The town is also the highest point in the province east of the Rockies at 1210 metres.

SLAVE LAKE

Nicknamed the "Jewel of the North," its surrounding countryside is brimming with natural wonders—Alberta's largest recreational lake, sandy beaches, hiking trails, abundant wildlife, boat launches and incredible fishing.

SYLVAN LAKE

One of the largest inland lakes in the country, it claims to have the only inland lighthouse between the West Coast and the Great Lakes. The town has been famous as a sandy-beach resort since 1904.

WETASKIWIN

Known as the "Car Capital of Canada," the town boasts more car sales per capita than anywhere else in the nation. It is also known for the Edmonton International Raceway, central Alberta's only paved stock-car racetrack. The Reynolds Alberta Museum is also found here, one of North America's largest collections of antique and classic cars.

DID YOU KNOW?

Wetaskiwin is home to Canada's Aviation Hall of Fame, founded in 1973.

Aerospace is still a major industry in Alberta. Sixty companies employ over 4500 highly skilled workers in engineering, technical or management expertise, contributing about $675 million to the provincial economy in 2003.

WAINWRIGHT

Known as Canada's "Bison Capital," its Town Clock, erected in 1925, is the only free-standing war monument of its kind in Canada.

WHITECOURT

This town is known as Canada's "Snowmobiling Capital."

BIG STUFF

*People are becoming increasingly fascinated by large structures on
the side of the road. Some stop to take a look, while others detour
miles out of their way to spot one. It's a growing phenomenon that
catches on wherever people have to drive long distances and don't
have much taste in classic architectural design. But hey, what
a wonderful world we live in, when a massive pink shrimp or
an oversized kangaroo can brighten up someone's day.*

Nineteen Big Ones

Alberta claims 19 world records for the very largest of these
lumps of roadside art. It would take about a month to visit all of
Alberta's en route attractions, so here are just the highlights.

The World's Largest Mallard Duck

This big bird nests at Andrew, weighs 1 tonne and has a
wingspan of 7.2 metres. This fibreglass quacker commemorates
the real birds that flock to the surrounding wetland areas.

The World's Largest Beaver

The beast is 5.5 metres long, 4.6 metres high, weighs 1.35
tonnes and sits on a 6.1-metre-wide log. It's found in the town
of Beaverlodge, which is also known as the "Gateway to
Monkman's Pass."

Angus Shaw, the Fur Trader

He's carved out of wood and towers 7 metres tall outside the
town of Bonnyville. Angus was the first European to visit the
area in the 1700s.

Pinto MacBean

He can be found at Bow Island and stands more than 4 metres high. MacBean sports a cowboy hat and bandana to welcome newcomers to the town, which is known as the "Bean Capital of the West." Also at Bow Island is the World's Largest (Golf) Putter.

Brian's Bull

Brownvale brandishes a bucking brahma bull ridden by an out-sized Brian Mulroney (honestly!), the prime minister at the time the bull was built in 1986 as an exhibit for the Alberta Pavilion at the World Expo in Vancouver.

Susie, the World's Largest Softball

Susie landed in Chauvin and commemorates the town's annual softball tournament.

The Biggest Piggy Bank in the World

You can fill it up at the town of Coleman, and all proceeds go to the local Lion's Club. Called "Ten Ton Toots," the bank is made out of an old steam engine that hauled over 4.5 million tonnes of coal from surrounding underground mines.

The World's Largest Chuckwagon

Take it for a ride at the village of Dewberry. The wagon is one and a half times the dimensions of a real one and is fully functional, so it's entered every year in the town's annual chuckwagon competition.

The World's Largest Lamp

This monument burns bright at 12.8 metres tall and lights up the town of Donalda, which has an oil lamp museum.

The World's Largest Dinosaur, "Dino 2000"

She's having a roaring good time standing outside Drumheller's Tourist Information Centre and is a colossal 26 metres high, 46 metres long and weighs in at 66 tonnes. A flight of stairs inside the body (106 steps) leads visitors into Dino's mouth, where eight people at a time can look out over the Badlands. Dino overshadows Dini, the town's other T-rex, which grew to a mere 6.1 metres high and 10.7 metres long.

The 30 other dinosaurs scattered around Drumheller are also the work of Trygve "Tig" Seland. They originally roamed around the specially built Prehistoric Park and had a 9.1-metre statue of Jesus built to watch over them. Christ's "flock" of dinosaurs was removed when the rest of the park was closed in 1995, but Jesus is still there.

The Dove of Peace

This metal monument looks like an airplane, but it pacifies Edmonton because it was built as an outdoor cathedral for the visit of Pope John Paul II in 1984. The bird has a wingspan of 17 metres. A time capsule buried underneath will be opened on the 200th anniversary of the Edmonton Catholic School District.

The World's Largest Western Boot

This monster-sized footwear was stitched up out of fibreglass in Edmonton in 1989 at a cost of $200,000 to promote the shoe factory it stands in front of. The company is gone, but the boot remains, and there are plans to add another 2 metres to the boot's current height of 12 metres (that's four storeys).

The World's Largest Bee

It's just under 7 metres long and buzzes around Falher, Canada's honey capital. The region has more than 48,000 colonies of honeybees, which produce an annual average of 4500 tonnes of honey.

The World's Largest Wagon Wheel and Pick

This statue rolls around Fort Assiniboine.

The World's Largest Pyrogy

Otherwise known as a Ukranian dumpling, the pyrogy is spiked onto a giant fork, stands 6.2 metres tall and weighs 2700 kilograms. It was stuffed in the town of Glendon out of fibreglass and steel.

Trumpeter Swan

The bird is Grande Prairie's official symbol, so one was built flying 3 metres tall at the city's gateway. Half of Canada's migrating geese spend about six months of the year here. The city also has a giant silver sundial for telling the time.

A Wind Gauge

Lethbridge, Alberta's windiest city, hosts this guy. It was inaugurated in 1985 for the city's centennial. The 1.3-metre-wide ball used as the gauge hangs off a 5.5-metre-high frame.

The World's Largest Sundial

This monument outshines them all at Lloydminster. But even more significant are the four massive border posts that run along Meridian Avenue. These 30-metre-tall pillars demarcate the fourth meridian of the of the Dominion Land Survey (or 110° west longitude) and the Alberta-Saskatchewan border, which splits the city in two—the western half of town lies in Alberta, the eastern half in Saskatchewan.

The Cream Can

The town of Markerville is known for this 4.6-metre-high monument that pays homage to the Icelandic settlers who built up the town around a successful creamery business.

The Saamis Tipi

The tipi was first erected for the 1988 Calgary Winter Olympics as a symbol of Canada's Native heritage. Saamis is the Blackfoot word for the eagle-tailfeather headdress, or "medicine hat," worn by medicine men. At 65.5 metres, it towered above the Olympic flame during the opening and closing ceremonies. It was relocated to Medicine Hat after the Olympics—quite a shift considering it weighs 800 tonnes.

The World's Biggest Ukrainian Sausage

The town of Mundare minced this monument to commemorate the kielbasa Ukrainian sausage—the vital ingredient of the local Stawnichy's Meat Processing sausage factory's success. The sausage was built on the factory's 50th birthday at a cost of about $120,000 and can withstand 160 kilometre per hour winds.

The World's Largest Bucking Saddle Bronc and Rider
It's called "The Legacy" and is saddled up in Ponoka.

The World's Largest Oil Derrick

This structure stands 51 metres tall in the town of Redwater.

Sangudo's Sundial
The 6.4-metre-tall sundial that looks like a grain elevator marks the entrance site to the village of Sangudo. The angle of the upper roof slope was built at 54° 54", Sangudo's latitude north, which means the time indicated is local solar time. Sangudo Solar Time is, on average, about 40 minutes behind MST or 1 hour and 40 minutes behind MDT.

The World's Largest Badminton Racquet
It hit the streets of St. Albert near Edmonton in 2000. It's 4.3 metres tall, weighs 225 kilograms and was built to raise awareness of the game by an avid fan.

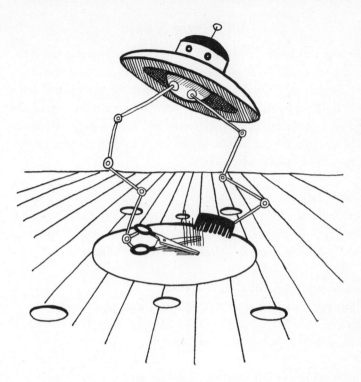

UFO Data Centre and Landing Pad

There's a whole other world to be found in the town of St. Paul. The landing pad spans 12 metres in diameter. The plaque reads: *Republic of St. Paul (Stargate Alpha). The area under the World's First UFO Landing Pad was designated international by the Town of St. Paul as a symbol of our faith that mankind will maintain the outer universe free from national wars and strife. That future travel in space will be safe for all intergalactic beings, all visitors from Earth or otherwise are welcome to this territory and to the Town of St. Paul.*

The World's Largest Mushrooms
They sprouted at the village of Vilna and are 6 metres high with mushroom heads 3 metres wide.

A Grizzly Swan

The town of Swan Hills celebrates its name with a massive steel sculpture of a 317-kilogram swan, protecting her nest of five eggs (weighing 159 kilograms) from a massive grizzly bear that weighs 498 kilograms. Swans can be vicious, sure, but what's the betting on whether the big guy will win? It took over 500 hours to piece together the 20,000 segments of steel that make up the statue and cost around $35,000.

Taber's Tallest
Cornstalks reaching up to 11 metres high tuft the land at Taber, Alberta's corn capital and site of the famous annual Cornfest. The town's nickname is "Market Garden of Alberta."

Sammy and Samantha, the Potatoes
These taters look chipper welcoming visitors to the town of Vauxhall, also known as the "Potato Capital of the West." Each of the fibreglass taters is 2.1 metres tall.

The World's Largest Pysanka (Easter Egg)
This commemorative monument is also a weather vane. It was built as a tribute from Vegreville's predominantly Ukrainian immigrants to the North-West Mounted Police on the latter's centenary anniversary in 1973, as a gift of gratitude for keeping the settlement safe for over 100 years.

Enterprising Vulcan

The town of Vulcan cashed in on the fame of the *Star Trek* cult TV and movie series. Its replica of the *Starship Enterprise* is just under 10 metres tall, 3 metres wide and weighs 5 tonnes. It is best seen lit up at night. There is also a Star Trek Station that serves as the town's information centre and gift shop. Vulcan's other claim to fame is that it is also known as the "Wheat Capital of Canada."

WEIRD PLACE NAMES

Whatever Your Mood, There's a Place in Alberta to Suit

For a feel good, fancy a frolic in Makepeace, Paradise Valley or Happy Hollow? Or, for those down days, take a trip to Quarrel, Gloomy Creek or Dismal Creek.

HEAD-SMASHED-IN BUFFALO JUMP

The place gets its name from the tragedy of a young brave who got much too close to the action. The young man wanted to witness the bison being driven over the cliff and crashing to their deaths in the tradition of First Nations communal hunting jumps. He must have thought his vantage point on a stone ledge on the cliff was safe, but the bison just kept on coming and coming—so many of them that he was pinned against the cliff wall and eventually crushed to death.

☞ Head-Smashed-In is North America's oldest and largest bison-hunting jump site. The system of lanes used to drive the bison over the edge is the largest in existence. Alberta's first-ever professional archeological dig took place there in 1948.

LISTENING MOUNTAIN

This land feature looks like an ear, hence its name.

DEAD MAN FLATS

The tale behind this name is one of fratricide. Jean Marret was murdered by his brother François, who finally lost his cool because Jean hadn't paid him any wages for two years. François threw the body into the Bow River, hoping his brother's ghost wouldn't haunt him. He was acquitted on grounds of insanity, claiming the voices of his dead parents told him to kill his brother because he was evil.

GRANDE CACHE
In French, this means a big, hidden stash. It was the place fur hunters would hide away all the pelts they'd collected so they could retrieve them after winter.

NISKU
Stanislaw Sarnecki was head of a community of 20 families from Poland when CPR representatives asked him to name the nearby station. Stanislaw, who was still learning English, misunderstood and thought they wanted him to describe the land, so he said *nisko tu*, meaning "low, flat land here." To the representatives, it translated to "Nisku."

MEDICINE HAT
This city takes its name from the Blackfoot word "saamis," which translates as "the medicine man's hat." The town's main claim to fame is the Medicine Hat Pottery Company, later renamed Medalta Potteries Ltd., which by 1975 was producing 75% of all Canadian clay products.

ST. ALBERT
St. Albert isn't named after the province, but after the first Catholic missionary, Father Albert Lacombe, who established a mission there in 1861. Father Lacombe was trusted by and advocated for First Nations people. His role as a peacemaker allowed the first railway to be built, and he promoted the signing of treaties with the First Nations. Without his work, the new homesteaders wouldn't have stood a chance in this wild frontier.

LACOMBE'S MEMORIAL PIG
In 1957, the "Lacombe hog" became the first breed of livestock to be developed in Canada, the product of 10 years of swine breeding research at the Canadian Department of Agriculture Experimental Farm, located in the town of Lacombe.

BIG MOVIES SHOT IN ALBERTA

For a big land with a tiny population, Alberta has produced its fair share of superstars and been visited by some.

Movie Mecca

A total of 237 major feature films have been shot in Alberta (either selected scenes or in their totality), some homegrown, some for the UK, Japan, India, France and Germany, but most for United States—because locations here are cheaper. Since 1999, 100 films have been shot in the province, and every year more made-in-Alberta movies are hitting the screens internationally.

Silent Start

Filmmaking in Alberta goes back to Nell Shipman's *Back to God's Country* (1919), shot at Lesser Slave Lake.

Second Wave

Next came Paramount Pictures *The Emperor Waltz* (1946), shot in Jasper by one of the world's most respected directors, Billy Wilder, and starring Bing Crosby and Joan Fontaine. Bing loved Jasper so much he kept coming back and even set up a golf tournament there.

Train Ticket

In 1948, Twentieth Century Fox filmed *Pacific*, a story about the Canadian Pacific Railway, in Banff.

Running River

The River of No Return, produced by Twentieth Century Fox, was shot in 1953. It features the landscape of Jasper National Park and actors Marilyn Monroe and Robert Mitchum.

Avalanche!

In 1954, the Columbia Icefields played the part of Alaska's Chilkoot Pass in *The Far Country*, starring James Stewart and Ruth Roman. At one point during filming, the director was convinced to move from a site his Canadian crew thought dangerous, and half an hour after they cleared out, an avalanche hit.

Provincial First

In 1959, Alberta's first homegrown feature film, *Wings of Chance*, was shot in Edmonton and Jasper thanks to Alberta producer Larry Matanksi. The story is about a bush pilot who crashes in the Alberta wilderness.

Never Work with Animals...

Disney studios built a "wildlife studio" in Kananaskis Country in 1960. Animal sequences could be shot there and then later used in various movies.

Studio Reserves

Little Big Man, starring Faye Dunaway and Dustin Hoffman, was filmed in 1969 at the Stoney Indian Reserve in Morley.

A Great Western

In 1975, director Robert Altman shot *Buffalo Bill and the Indians*, starring Hollywood greats Paul Newman and Burt Lancaster, again at the Stoney Indian Reserve. Morley's own Frank Kaquitts played Sitting Bull.

Dustbowl Drama

Why Shoot the Teacher, filmed in 1976, was a highly acclaimed, truly Canadian film about a slice of prairie life during the Dust Bowl and the Great Depression of the 1930s. It was shot in Drumheller. Many of the co-stars were amateurs and natives of the prairie where it was filmed.

Long, Very Long Days in Lethbridge
In 1976, *Days of Heaven*, starring Sam Shepard, Richard Gere and Brooke Adams, was shot in Lethbridge over a span of two years because director Terry Malick wanted to shoot in all four seasons. The gamble paid off and the film won an Oscar for best photography.

The Great White North Goes Quiet
In 1980, Fort McMurray was the location for *Silence of the North*, based on a true story of wilderness pioneering. It starred Ellen Burstyn and Tom Skerritt.

Is It a Bird?
No, it's *Superman II* and *III*. Both movies had segments shot in Calgary, the Columbia Icefields and High River, with additional filming at Niagara Falls. In *Superman III*, in the opening sequence, Calgary is used to represent downtown Metropolis.

First Gold Nation
Running Brave, shot in 1982 for Walt Disney, was filmed in Drumheller and Edmonton and starred Robby Benson. It follows the story of Sioux Billy Mills, who won gold at the 1964 Tokyo Olympics.

Mad in the Mall
The Running Man, made in 1987, saw Arnold Schwarzenegger running around West Edmonton Mall.

Dead in its Tracks?

In 1988, *Dead Bang,* starring Don Johnson, nearly didn't happen because Johnson had skipped bail in Canada a few years previously for hitting a Mountie while drunk on another shoot.

Wheeler's Drive
In 1989, *Bye Bye Blues* was directed by Edmonton-born Anne Wheeler, one of Canada's most successful female directors. Stunning scenes of the Alberta landscape helped the movie score four Genie wins and 10 international nominations.

As Above, So Below
Also in 1989, the Morley Reserve was the location for the $60 million Japanese epic *Heaven and Earth.* Seven hundred wild horses had to be broken to saddle; 5000 suits of samurai armour had to be made; and a cast of 400 hundred actors and 3000 extras had to be assembled.

Brad's First Visit

Brad Pitt's first visit to Edmonton, in 1994, was to star in *Legends of the Fall* alongside Anthony Hopkins and Aidan Quinn. It was filmed in Calgary and on the Morley Reserve.

Mush!

In 2002, *Snow Dogs* starred Cuba Gooding Jr. and James Coburn in a movie about a Miami dentist who inherits a team of sled dogs. It was directed by Brian Levant and filmed in Calgary and Canmore. By the way, the word "mush" has nothing to do with wet snow; it's from the French word *marchons*, meaning "move on!"

Alberta Oscar

The Unforgiven, made in the province in 1992, was directed by and starred Clint Eastwood. Other notable Hollywood heroes in the cast included Morgan Freeman, Gene Hackman and Richard Harris. The town of Big Whisky was built at the Cartwright Ranch in 43 days. The film was only the third western in history to win an Oscar for best picture, and it won three others as well.

☛ **The rainmakers.** Most of the rain in the film was specially created because the location was experiencing a dry spell, though the snowfall that is featured when William Munney (Clint Eastwood) is recovering from his beating was unexpected (and unscripted).

☛ **The bootmakers.** Clint's boots in the movie were the same as those he wore in the 1959 TV series *Rawhide*.

Extraordinary ex-Bond

The League of Extraordinary Gentlemen, starring Sean Connery, who played James Bond in many 007 movies, was made in 2003 in Calgary and surrounding areas.

Prairie Science

The sci-fi thriller *X2*, filmed in 2003, starred Halle Berry, Hugh Jackman and Sir Ian Mackellan. When the production arrived in Alberta to film the Arctic snow scenes, there wasn't any white stuff, so snow had to be created specially for the film.

Black Day for Filming
Same thing happened in the winter of 2004—no snow when it came time to shoot *Christmas Blessings* on the streets of Edmonton.

Black Movie on Main
The 2004 horror flick *Santa's Slay* was filmed on Wetaskiwin's historic Main Street.

Brad Pitt's Second Visit

The hottie returned to Alberta in the summer of 2005 to star in *The Assassination of Jesse James*, which was filmed extensively at Fort Edmonton Park. Photos of Brad and girlfriend Angelina Jolie were taken of the couple at West Edmonton Mall by two Edmonton waitresses, who then sold them to the world's tabloids, eager to prove the two were now officially a couple. The pictures fetched USD $26,000 from publications in the U.S. and Canada alone.

Another Great North
Andy Thomson and Patricia Philips set up Edmonton's Great North Productions, which was at one time the biggest independent producer of TV in western Canada, responsible for hit series such as *Jake and the Kid* and *Acorn! The Nature Nut*. Its doors were closed by parent company Alliance Atlantis in 2004.

Award-Winning!

Hollywood heartthrobs Heath Ledger and Jake Gyllenhal took a massive career risk by playing homosexual cowboys in *Brokeback Mountain* (2005). The movie, co-produced by Alberta Film Entertainment, was filmed in Fort Macleod and Calgary and used the Rockies of the Kananaskis as its stunning backdrop. Director Ang Lee (*Crouching Tiger, Hidden Dragon; Sense and Sensibility*) described it as the best shooting experience of his career so far. The movie cleaned up at award ceremonies all over the world, including four wins out of seven Golden Globe nominations—one for Best Picture, Drama.

ALBERTANS WITH STARS IN THEIR EYES

Here's a quick list of famous people in popular culture who have something to do with the province...even if it's only a tiny little bit.

Kong from Cardston

The lovely actress Fay Wray, who played the beauty King Kong was besotted by, was a native of Cardston in southern Alberta.

The Singing Politician

He's a senator these days, but Tommy Banks was once the face of big band music in Edmonton. He owned and operated Century II Studios, has acted in films and, for a dozen years, hosted *The Tommy Banks Show.*

Gay Times

Eric McCormack, who stars as the gay attorney in the hit TV series *Will & Grace*, was born in Toronto, raised in Calgary and studied at the Banff Centre for the Arts. Now a dual citizen of the U.S. as well as Canada, Eric sang both the American and Canadian national anthems at the 2004 NHL All-Star Game in Minnesota.

Alberta Songbird Migrates

Joni Mitchell is probably one of the most successful ever
Canadian singer-songwriters. She was born in Fort Macleod and
grew up in Saskatchewan. Inducted into the Juno Hall of Fame
in 1981, she was the first Canadian woman inductee into the
U.S. Rock and Roll Hall of Fame. In 2002, she was appointed
a Companion of the Order of Canada and received a Grammy
Lifetime Achievement Award.

The Lesbian Vegetarian with a Velvet Voice

k.d. lang, another singer-songwriter, was born in Consort and
studied music at Red Deer College. When she made it big in
the charts, the town proudly erected a signpost: "Consort:
Home of k.d. lang," only to take it down again when she
declared herself a vegetarian and a lesbian. All was forgiven at
the province's centenary celebrations, however, when she head-
lined Alberta's 100th birthday concert.

King of Country

George Fox was born in the foothills of the Rocky Mountains and has risen to many peaks in the country music business—his awards include four CCMA trophies for country male vocalist, three Junos and five gold records. Other highlights include four CBC television specials and 23 top-ten hits.

Build It and They Will Come

Edmonton-born author W.P. Kinsella's book *Shoeless Joe* inspired the Hollywood movie *Field of Dreams*, starring Kevin Costner. Kinsella's work has sold millions of books. It has also won him countless fans, not the least of which was the jury of the Stephen Leacock Medal for Humour, which he won in 1987. And in 1994, Kinsella was inducted into the Order of Canada.

Queen of Country

Singer-songwriter Terri Clark is one of North America's most successful country and western singers. Born in Montréal, she grew up in Medicine Hat and now lives in Tennessee.

Fox's Family

Actor Michael J. Fox was born Michael Andrew Fox on June 9, 1961, in Edmonton. Michael is most famous for his role as Alex P. Keaton on NBC's *Family Ties,* which ran for seven years from 1982 to 1989. In 1991, he was diagnosed with Parkinson's disease, and a decade later established a foundation in his name to combat the disease.

Glue-Sniffing Funny Man

Actor Leslie Nielsen, star of comedy hit movies such as the *Airplane!* series (where he sniffs glue to alleviate pre-crash stress) and the unforgettable movie *Naked Gun*, was born in the Yukon and grew up in Edmonton. His first media job was as a disc jockey in Calgary before he moved to Toronto to attend the Lorne Green Academy of Radio Arts.

Winds Still Blowing Strong Every Year

Ian Tyson, singer and author of "Four Strong Winds," one of
Canada's best-known folk songs (which is always sung to close
every Edmonton Folk Festival), lives on a ranch in Longview,
near Calgary. He also owns the town's cappuccino bar.

Fitness Queen

Edmonton's Cynthia Kereluk, winner of the 1984 Miss Canada
Pageant, became part of the TV fitness wave that swept North
America. At its height in the late 1980s, her show *Everyday
Workout* was seen by 42 million households.

No Nickels to Rub Together

The members of Nickelback, one of Canada's most popular
bands, were born and bred in Hanna. Fed up with playing cover
versions of other people's songs, singer-guitarist Chad Kroeger
wrote a few tunes, borrowed $4000 from his stepfather (because
the band didn't have a nickel between them), recorded an album
and, with the band, went to live in Vancouver. The album was
picked up by big labels, and now, three records later, the band
plays to millions and earns millions.

Jann's Tongue in Cheek

Singer-songwriter Jann Arden was born in Calgary and ranks
in the top five of Canadian artists. A philosophical thinker and
confirmed self-deprecator, Arden's talent, wit and a bit of good
luck saved her from a life of booze and bumming around the
Calgary music scene. Her first album won two Junos in 1993
for Best Solo Performer and Best Video. The second album sold
six-times platinum in Canada and 500,000 in the U.S. More
Junos came in 1995 for Female Vocalist of the Year, Songwriter
of the Year and Single of the Year.

Honourary Albertan

Comedy actor Eugene Levy was honoured with the Distinguished Achievement Award by the Alberta Motion Picture Industry at its annual ceremony in 2005. Although not an Albertan, he was instrumental in the production of Second City Theatre, based in Edmonton, and its spinoff *Second City TV (SCTV)*—the hit series of edgy and irreverent comedy shows. The series ran on North American networks from 1976 to 1981 and rivalled the popularity of *Saturday Night Live*. It was picked up by NBC in 1981. *SCTV* launched the careers of other famous Canuck comics Joe Flaherty, Andrea Martin, Catherine O'Hara, John Candy, Martin Short and Andrew Alexander, among others.

The World's Worst Movie

Director Arthur Hiller was born in Edmonton in 1932 and attended the Victoria School of Performing Arts. His credits include the blockbuster *Silver Streak,* shot in Alberta, and he directed five actors in Oscar-nominated performances. But he would never want to be credited with a movie he walked away from that ended up winning a Golden Raspberries for the World's Worst Movie. *An Alan Smithee Film: Burn Hollywood Burn* is about a Hollywood director fighting to take his name off the credits. Hiller did exactly the same thing in real life (one of only 30 cases granted by the Director's Guild of America), so the film is credited to Alan Smithee.

Hiller was honoured with a star on the Toronto Walk of Fame in 2002 and make an Officer of the Order of Canada in 2006.

My Big, Fat Greek Party

Yianni's Greek restaurant in Edmonton became legendary in the 1980s for hosting wild parties for the Edmonton Oilers. In 2005, the family's restaurants became famous again in a six-part TV documentary-reality series *The Family Restaurant*.

FAMOUS VISITORS

Sanctuary for Sitting Bull

The Big Chief fled to Alberta to avoid the U.S. Army after killing General George Custer and his 265 men at the Battle of Little Big Horn. He and his 500 Sioux warriors survived for five years without any help from the Canadians until 1881, when Sitting Bull led his starving people back home.

Kipling's Quickie

Famed author Rudyard Kipling stopped in Medicine Hat during a trip across Canada in 1907, noted that the city had a plentiful supply of natural gas directly below it and said the city had— among other virtues—"all hell for a basement."

King of Dance's Prairie Debut

Fred Astaire made his professional dancing debut at age 12 in a touring stage show that played Calgary's Sherman Grand Theatre in 1912.

First Royal Visitors

In 1901, the Duke and Duchess of Cornwall and York made the first royal visit to Alberta. The first reigning monarchs to visit Alberta were George VI and Queen Elizabeth (later the Queen Mother) on June 2, 1939. It was also their first royal visit abroad as king and queen.

DID YOU KNOW?

George's brother, King Edward VIII, who abdicated the British crown and became the Duke of Windsor, also visited Alberta. He liked it so much he bought the E.P. Ranch in southern Alberta, which he owned for 42 years. Apparently Mrs. Simpson thought the place was frightful and never came to visit.

Top Royal

Queen Elizabeth II has visited four times, in 1959, 1973, 1978 and 2005, making her the monarch with the most visits.

The People's Princess on the Prairies
In 1983, Princess Diana and Prince Charles toured the province. One of their official duties was to open the World University Games in Edmonton's Commonwealth Stadium.

Other Royal Visits

1967 The Prince and Princess of Japan pop over to attend the grand opening of the Nikka Yuko Japanese Garden.

1984 Pope John Paul II. (The bench he sat on is commemorated at Elk Island National Park.)

1985 Crown Prince Vajiralongkorn of Thailand.

1985 Queen Elizabeth, the Queen Mother, 46 years after her first visit.

1987 King Olav V of Norway.

1988 A bumper royal year because of the Calgary Olympics. Visitors included Queen Beatrix of the Netherlands, King Juan Carlos of Spain, King Carl XVI Gustaf of Sweden and Prince Rainier of Monaco.

1989 Just one visit from King Hussein of Jordan.

THE WINNINGEST ALBERTANS

The First Albertan to Ever Compete in the Olympics

Alex Decoteau of Edmonton was the first-ever Albertan to compete for Team Canada in Sweden's 1912 Summer Olympics. He ran the 5000 metres but didn't win a medal.

Hockeylympics
Edmonton's Waterloo Mercurys won Olympic gold in ice hockey in 1952 in Oslo, Norway.

DID YOU  KNOW?

The Olympics have only been held in Canada twice—the Summer Olympics in Montréal 1976 and the Calgary Winter Games in 1988. The Winter Games return to Vancouver in 2010.

Synchro Gold

Michelle Cameron became the first Albertan to win an Olympic gold medal for synchronized swimming at the 1988 Seoul Olympics. Her husband Alan Coulter holds two records—the shortest man to play for the Canadian Olympic volleyball team, but with 735 international matches under his belt, he is also the man who has played more times for his country than anyone else.

 The Olympic Speed Skating Oval in Calgary was North America's first covered speed-skating arena.

Albertan Athenians

Edmonton cyclist Lori-Ann Muenzer and Calgary gymnast Kyle Shewfelt won gold medals at the 2004 Athens Olympics. Kyle was the first Canadian ever to win a medal in artistic gymnastics—he won gold on the floor exercise.

 The world's largest Olympic museum is the Olympic Hall of Fame in Calgary.

Museum Move

The Alberta Sports Hall of Fame and Museum moved to its new permanent location near Heritage Ranch in Red Deer in 2002.

Double Winner

Catriona Le May Doan, who adopted Calgary as her home, won speed skating gold medals in 1998 and 2002, and her 500-metre time of 37.22 seconds, set in December 2001, still stands as the world record.

Canada's First Medal on Home Soil

Banff's Karen Percy-Lowe (married to Edmonton Oilers general manager Kevin Lowe) did it for Team Canada, winning two bronzes in the 1988 Winter Games for downhill skiing and super giant slalom.

Salty Bonanza
At the 2002 Salt Lake City Winter Olympics, Canadians won 17 medals—the most Team Canada has ever won.

Legendary Bobsleighers
Calgary's Pierre Lueders, won bobsleigh gold at the 1998 Nagano Games with brakeman Dave McEachern. Amazingly, the gold was actually a tie with the Italians—both teams scored exactly the same cumulative time after four heats, so for the first time ever, two teams shared the gold.

Women's Soccer Champs—Nearly

At Edmonton's Commonwealth Stadium, the Canadian women's soccer team reached international prominence in 2002 at the inaugural FIFA Under-20s in the Women's World Cup for the Under-20s. The Canucks lost to their archrivals, the American team. A massive crowd of 30,000 attended the game.

Show-Jumping Spruces Compete for Top Spot

Spruce Meadows is ranked either first- or second-best show jumping venue in the world depending on the reviewers. Its main rival for the title is a facility in Aachen, Germany. Spruce Meadows is open year-round and holds both indoor and outdoor competitions.

John Cormier from Red Deer was the first Albertan to swim the English Channel. He did it in 1988.

Canada's First-Ever World Cup Downhill Ski Event

This event took place in 1980 at Lake Louise.

DID YOU  KNOW?

Kurt Browning is listed in the *Guinness Book of World Records* as the first skater in the world to land a quadruple jump in competition. Kurt was born in Rocky Mountain House and has won four World Figure Skating Championships since his first victory in 1989. In 1994, he became one of the youngest citizens to be awarded the Order of Canada.

Sports Quiz

Name the international sporting events held in Alberta in 1978, 1983, 1988, 2001 and 2005.

1978 Commonwealth Games, Edmonton: elite Commonwealth athletes compete.

1983 World University Games, Edmonton: the first time these games were staged in North America.

1988 Winter Olympics, Calgary: Canada wins five medals—two silver, three bronze.

2001 IAAF World Athletics Championships, Edmonton

2005 World Masters Games, Edmonton: Olympics for the over-35s. Edmonton's Sandy Jacobson won gold in both the 10-kilometre race and the half marathon.

CHAMPION OF CHAMPIONS

Wayne Gretzky is probably one of the most famous Albertans of all time, even though he was born in Brantford, Ontario. In fact, Wayne's first two professional goals were scored against the Edmonton Oilers.

Virgin NHLers

Gretzky played for the Edmonton Oilers the very first year the team joined the National Hockey League in 1979, when they amazed everyone and made it to the Stanley Cup playoffs.

Big Hitter

In his second season, Gretzky scored more points than any other player in the league, and continued to do so for the next six years.

The Champion Captain

Gretzky was captain of the Oilers when the team won its first-ever Stanley Cup in 1984, the first of five the team won over the next six years (1984, 1985, 1987, 1988 and 1990).

DID YOU KNOW?

In 1981, Gretzky surpassed one of the game's most cherished records—"50 goals in 50 games." But he did it in only the 39th game of the season. In total, Gretzky holds 42 NHL records.

Not-So-Great Gretzky

Edmonton Oilers owner Peter Pocklington swapped Gretzky and another Oilers player for two members of the Los Angeles Kings team and $15 million cash in what became known as "the Trade." Both were seen as traitors by the fans—Pocklington's effigy was burned in the streets, and Gretzky's popularity in Canada sank.

Gretzky's November to Remember

In 2003, Gretzky took to the ice one last time to help celebrate the Edmonton Oilers 25th anniversary as an NHL team. They played and lost 4–3 to the Montréal Canadiens. The Heritage Classic was the first NHL game to be played outdoors, and November temperatures were as low as –15°C. None of the 55,000 fans will ever forget that.

Greek Gretzky

After the Heritage Classic defeat, the Oilers reunited for one last meal at Yianni Psalios's Greek restaurant, Koutouki, in Edmonton. Yianni's was the place the Oilers always held legendary parties after each Stanley cup win in the 1980s…but in 1988, they had such a good time, they left the Cup behind, and Yianni had to take it home with him for safekeeping.

Another Great Ice Man

Alberta's other hockey legend is Hanna native Lanny McDonald. Apart from being remembered for his really big all-star ginger moustache, Lanny played for teams in Lethbridge and Medicine Hat before breaking records as a member of the Toronto Maple Leafs—a consecutive 40 goals every season from 1976 to 1979. Returning to Alberta to join the Calgary Flames in 1988–89, McDonald registered his 1000th career point and scored his 500th goal against the New York Islanders.

LAW AND DISORDER

Two Alberta Laws Still on the Books

"Wooden logs may not be painted."
"You may never use dice to play craps."

The Penalty for Being in Texas

Albertan Stanley Faulder was executed by lethal injection in Texas in June 1999, under the watch of Governor George W. Bush. Faulder was the first Canadian to be executed in the U.S. since 1952, after serving 22 years on death row for murder. Convicted in 1977, he had been on death row for more than 15 years before the U.S. even informed the Canadian government that he was in jail. Ironically, in 1965, Faulder had saved the life of Jeannine Janusz after a near fatal car accident in an Alberta blizzard.

DID YOU KNOW?

In 2003, the overall crime rate in Alberta was lower than the rates in other western provinces for the 11th consecutive year. The Territories have the highest crime rates. However, the provincial crime rate is going up. Albertans committed 8% more property crime, 2% more violent crimes and 15% more car thefts in 2003.

Manitoba Murders

Of all Canadian cities, Regina is the most likely place to get murdered, with five homicides committed for every 100,000 people. Winnipeg comes next with 4.9, followed by Edmonton with 3.4. Québec City is the least likely place to be murdered, with 0.8 homicides per 100,000 people. Calgary ranks in the middle of the tables at 1.9.

Bonnie and Canuck Clyde

Florence Lassandro was the only woman ever to be executed in Alberta. She was hanged on May 2, 1923, along with her lover Emilio Picariello, a notorious bootlegger, for the murder of a police officer. Not since 1899 had a woman been executed in Canada.

DID YOU KNOW?

The Mounties who keep law and order in Alberta are known as K Division.

Rough Justice

In 1991, a 14-year-old boy opened fire with a .22-calibre rifle inside W.R. Myers High School in Taber, killing one boy and wounding another. During the court trial, the boy (who cannot be named) required surgery for a heart condition, discovered after his arrest. He had a stroke during the surgery, went into a coma and was left mentally impaired and speech defective. He served three years in prison for the shootings and was released in 2003.

MADE IN Alberta All Canada's RCMP dogs are trained at Bowden—the only police dog training college in the country.

Murderous Prisoners of War

The largest mass hanging in Canadian history since the Riel Rebellion in 1885 took place at the Medicine Hat prisoner-of-war camp in 1944 when four German prisoners were executed for murdering two other inmates.

Missing Women
Alberta's K Division police force is currently investigating 82 unsolved murders of women with "high-risk lifestyles."

Growing Concern for Police
The number of marijuana grow operations in Alberta is increasing so rapidly that the RCMP has made the crime's eradication one of its top priorities. They seized $71 million worth of plants in 2004. In one Camrose bust alone, police seized 10,000 plants.

Charge the Card Please, Officer

Calgary police busted a credit card fraud racket in 2002, and in doing so prevented an estimated $23 million dollars in illegal shopping.

Lost in the Ether
Police in Edmonton busted a methamphetamine lab in 2003 that was capable of pumping out $1 million worth of the drug daily. There was enough ether (the main ingredient) found among the evidence to knock out six city blocks if ignited. Meth users are the hardest to treat of all drug users, and more women use it than men.

Chasing the Shadow
Alberta's largest-ever Hells Angels operation ended in a 2000 "takedown" (police-speak for a raid). Operation SHADOW resulted in 213 drug-related charges for possession of large amounts class-A drugs and illegal firearms.

Gunning Down the Law

The deadliest attack on police officers in the last 120 years shocked the country in March 2005, when four Mounties were gunned down as they investigated a marijuana growing operation in the rural town of Mayerthorpe.

Mounties Murdered

☛ August 1920: Constable Ernest Usher, 26, was shot and killed while trying to arrest train robbers at Bellewae.

☛ October 1935: Two RCMP officers, Constable George Harrison, 29, and Sergeant Thomas Wallace, 39, were killed when they spot-checked three brothers on the run who, just three days earlier, had slain two other Mounties in Manitoba.

☛ January 1985: Constable Allen Giesbrecht, 31, was shot dead while investigating a house scrawled with anti-RCMP slogans.

☛ January 1987: Special Constable Gordon Kowalczyk was called to investigate a man suspected of leaving a gas station without paying. The suspect shot the RCMP officer at point-blank range.

Law Quiz

Name the last person to be executed in Alberta and the year.

Robert Cook, at Fort Saskatchewan just a few minutes after midnight, on November 15, 1960, for the murder of his parents and five siblings, who he had shot and bludgeoned to death. Robert had been released from prison just days earlier.

FIRSTS

Alberta and its residents hold the records for...

Phone Records

Alberta's first premier, Alexander Cameron Rutherford, was instrumental in starting Edmonton's public telephone system, which holds two historical records. In 1908, the city's network became the first in North America to install automatic dial telephones, and it was also the first network to use 911 to summon emergency services.

The First Words Spoken on the Telephone in Alberta

On January 3, 1885, the Reverend Father Hippolyte from Leduc told St. Albert store owner H.W. McKenney: "We wish you all a very happy new year," over the phone. These very first words served as the first test for a newly completed line between the two towns.

Top Male Mountaineer

Laurie Skreslet of Calgary became the first Canadian to stand on top of Mount Everest, in 1982.

The First North American Woman to Climb Mount Everest
Alberta climber Sharon Wood of Canmore got to the top first in 1986.

A new style of fitted bedsheets that actually fit and stay put were the brainchild of Bonnyville farm girl Giselle Jubinville. She was turned down for a patent three times, but finally sold the idea to an American company for $1 million in 1990. Giselle now runs a holistic therapy centre.

The First Native Canadian Lieutenant-Governor
This accolade goes to Alberta's Ralph Steinhauer, a Cree from
Saddle Lake, appointed in 1974.

In 1986, Albertan Gail Greenough of
Edmonton became the first woman to win
a World Show Jumping Championship.

Canada's First-Ever Food Bank Started in Edmonton
It was necessitated by the economic hardship brought on by
the 1981 oil crisis. Since then, more than 650 similar volunteer
organizations have surfaced across the country, all following the
example set in Edmonton.

The First-Ever Community Leagues
Community leagues got their start in Edmonton in 1921. Today,
there are over 147 community leagues responsible for volunteer
organizations such as Neighbourhood Watch, school patrols, the
Community Police Radio Network and all sorts of associations
that run many of the province's recreational facilities.

The first municipal swimming pool in western Canada was built in Edmonton in 1922. First called the South Side Pool, it was renamed Queen Elizabeth Pool in 1939, in honour of the royal visit. A campaign got underway in 2005 to save the aging facility from developers and to raise cash for renovations.

The First Man to Ever Hold the Canadian Triple Crown of Auctioneering

In 2004, Dan Skeels of Rimbey took the three titles of Canadian Auctioneering Champion, World Champion Livestock Auctioneer and International Auctioneer Champion.

Freedom of the Press
In 1938, the *Edmonton Journal* became the first Alberta paper to win a Pulitzer Prize for opposing a law demanding that journalists divulge their sources. It's a fight that papers and governments fight out often, most recently in the UK and the U.S.

Canada's First Provincial Ombudsman

George McClellan, the retired RCMP commissioner, was the first man to get the job on April 6, 1967.

Alberta's first government-planned model town was Drayton Valley.

The First Motorized Fire Wagon

Calgary ratepayers bought the first engine in the province in 1909.

First Female Police Officer
Canada's first female cop was Edmonton's Annie Jackson in 1912.

DID YOU KNOW?

Edmonton is home to Alberta's first and only Nanaska Gurdwara Gurkish Temple, part of a global Gurkish network, where the city's Sikh community gather to pray.

It's All Up in the Air

The first person in Canada to be lifted into the air in a heavier-than-air machine was John Underwood of Stettler. In 1907, he spent 15 minutes, 3 metres up in the air on a homemade kite tied to the ground.

It's All Hot Air!
The first hot air balloon was brought to Alberta for the Calgary Exhibition in 1906.

 In 1941, an Edmonton streetcar piled high with books became North America's first travelling library.

Letters on the Move

In 1916, western Canada's first post office, the Palm Bay Post Office, was opened near Lake Athabasca.

Canada's First Public Broadcaster

The University of Alberta's CKUA Radio went on the air in 1927 to broadcast educational programs to schools—before schools even had radios.

BIGGEST, BETTER, BEST, OLDEST AND OTHER ALBERTA RECORDS

Centennial Celebrant

The oldest Albertan living on September 1, 2005, the province's 100th birthday, was 109-year-old Fong Ping Mah, who was born in China.

Original and Oldest

The oldest building in Alberta still on its original site is at Fort Victoria, halfway between Cold Lake and Edmonton. Owned by the Hudson's Bay Company, it has provided quarters for the company's clerks since 1864.

Edmonton's Great Western Garments sewed 75% of the Canadian uniforms used during World War II, making it the biggest textile factory in the nation. The firm was also famous as a manufacturer of Levi's Jeans until the company was outstitched by cheaper third-world imports and hung up its scissors in 2004.

Greatest Canadian Gear

The world's longest advertising poster was unveiled by O'Canada Gear at the Edmonton Aviation Heritage Society Hanger in September 2005. At 1.2 metres wide and over 300 metres long, it depicts historical events from the centennial year.

Royal Museums

Alberta is home to more museums with the "Royal" designation than any other province: the Royal Tyrrell Museum in Drumheller and the Royal Alberta Museum in Edmonton. The latter was formerly called the Provincial Museum but was renamed by royal designation in May 2005 during a visit by HRH Queen Elizabeth II. Ontario is home to the nation's only other regal displayer of antiquity, the Royal Ontario Museum.

DID YOU KNOW?

Redcliff, near Medicine Hat, is home to Alberta's last remaining drive-in movie theatre. Hey, fancy a kiss?

Any Old Anvil
The oldest operating blacksmith shop in Alberta and one of only two shops still standing on its original site is the Lacombe Blacksmith Shop.

Largest Ice Cream Sundae in the World
It took 20,100 kilograms of ice cream, 4260 kilograms of topping, 90 kilograms of whipped cream, 50 kilograms of peanuts and 50 kilograms of cherries to make this whopper at the Edmonton Convention Centre during Klondike Days in 1988.

Largest Loaf of Bread Ever Baked
This giant loaf was cooked up by the Calgary Italian Bakery and measured 2.75 metres by 1.5 metres, and weighed in at 1384 kilograms.

Can't Catch That!
Glen Gorbous of Drumheller is named by the *Guinness Book of World Records* as the man with the world's longest baseball throw—445 feet, 10 inches (135.9 metres). He was a major-league baseball pitcher, and his prize throw was achieved when he played with the St. Louis Cardinals in 1957.

E-TOWN MEETS COWTOWN

Calgarians, of course, have heard it all before—that Edmonton has bigger festivals, more theatre and better music than poor old Cowtown, stereotyped as a cultural backwater of oilmen and cowboys more interested in making money than watching men in tights.

Robert Remington
"File on Calgary: That was Then, This is Now"
Calgary Herald, December 1, 2003

Round One—Let the Games Begin

The seeds of rivalry between Alberta's two biggest cities were sown two months after the province's birth, when the ruling Liberal Party, elected in November 1905, chose Liberal-voting Edmonton in a 16–8 vote as the provincial capital instead of Conservative-voting Calgary. Edmonton was also Premier Rutherford's hometown.

Round Two—Eskimos Uncrushed by the Stampede

You just need to watch a football match between archrivals Calgary Stampeders and Edmonton Eskimos to praise the heavens they're all wearing safety helmets. But the Eskies *go go go* wayyyyyyy better than the Stampeders—Edmonton has won 13 out of the 23 Grey Cups they've played. Calgary has made it to fewer finals—only 11—and has won only five of those. The Toronto Argonauts, with 15 wins, are the only other team to have won more Cups than the Eskies.

Round Three—Edmonton Oilers Slicker than the Calgary Flames

Edmonton wins out at hockey, too, winning five of the six Stanley Cup finals they've played. The Calgary Flames have played three and won only once.

DID YOU  KNOW?

At the beginning of this millennium there were 35,494 more Calgarians than Edmontonians (1,037,093 to 1,001,599).

Edmonton is About 80 Years Older than Calgary
Edmonton was born in 1795, when the Hudson's Bay Company built Fort Edmonton as a trading fort on the site of the current Provincial Legislature building. Calgary didn't get going until 1875, when it was established as a North-West Mounted Police fort.

Edmonton Struck Gold...
Every year, Edmonton celebrates Klondike Days in one of the province's biggest summer festivals. This annual jamboree commemorates the event that first put Edmonton on the map—the Klondike Gold Rush of 1898, when 2000 gold prospectors flooded into town.

...and Calgary Struck, um, Cows

What put Calgary on the map was cows, and it's been that way ever since. First came the ranchers, who could lease massive wads of land for a pittance—100,000 acres (40,000 hectares) for just 1 penny per acre per year. (Things have gone up. The cost of leasing land in the Calgary area today is around $5 per ft^2 or $54 per m^2.) Just as the cows have grown fat on luscious prairie grasses and modern mechanized feedlots, Calgary has grown fat on the profits of growing into the centre of Canada's meat-packing and meat-marketing industries.

Edmonton may be Green...

Edmonton holds the record for having more parkland per capita than any other North American city.

...but Calgary Shines

Calgary has one of the highest levels of street lighting in North America. It is now refitting the bulbs in its lamps and will save around $2 million per year by reducing the wattage of 250- and 200-watt bulbs to 150- and 100-watt bulbs, as well as reducing greenhouse gas emissions by 16,000 tonnes a year.

Both Cities have Important Museums

While Calgary's Glenbow Museum holds the record for housing Canada's largest collection of Canadiana, Edmonton's has been given the royal seal of approval. The Provincial Museum and Archives was renamed the Royal Alberta Museum by Queen Elizabeth II on her 2005 centennial visit because she liked it so much. To be fair, the Queen didn't visit the Glenbow. Better luck next time, Cowtown.

The Same but Different

Each city has a high-rise revolving restaurant. Edmonton's circular eatery is to be found at the Crowne Plaza Hotel. Its rival can be visited at the Calgary Tower, which at 190.8 metres was the tallest building around until the 215-metre-high Petro-Canada building took over and is now the tallest skyscraper outside of Toronto. Both culinary circulars take exactly an hour to make one revolution.

Harking Back to Their Roots

Calgary and Edmonton were both named by the homesick men who first established them. Calgary comes from a Gaelic word meaning "clear water." The name was suggested by Sir James Macleod, who wanted a sentimental reminder of Calgary Bay, on the Isle of Mull in his ancestral Scotland. Edmonton also gets its name from Great Britain and is named for the area in London, England, that was home to Sir James Winter Lake, the deputy governor of the Hudson's Bay Company that built Fort Edmonton.

Teeming with Tea Drinkers

Edmonton is part of the London Borough of Enfield—that city's most northerly district. It has a population of 280,349 squeezed into just 82.2 km^2—a population density of 3411 km^2, compared to Canadian Edmonton's 974 per km^2. Calgary's population density is 1252.3 per km^2.

Not a Waste

Edmonton boasts North America's largest and most modern sustainable waste processing and research facilities. The Edmonton Waste Management Centre (EWMC) in the northeast of the city is the leader. The Edmonton Composting Facility, the destination of Edmonton's residential waste, is one of the largest composting facilities in the world. The city boasts that 60% of all residential waste is diverted away from landfill. Approximately 15% of residential waste is recycled, and 50% is composted.

Across Alberta, about 15% of consumer plastics are recycled. Since 1988, Edmonton and Red Deer residents can have their recyclables picked up at home. As a result, Edmonton recycles more waste per person than any other city in the world.

But Calgary Recycles Human Sewage into Farm Fertilizer!!
The city recycles 355,000 m³ of sewage daily, returning purified water to the Bow River and human-waste fertilizer to farms within a 60-kilometre radius of the city. The fields treated with the human-waste fertilizer are so much more productive than the untreated ones and their crops so abundant, that farmers are clamouring for the muck, which is given gratis.

Gas Goes Round and Round
An added benefit of Calgary's sewage reclamation process is the bio-gas that emanates from the sludge. It is captured and fed to four large generators, which generate 80% of all the electricity needed by the processing plants.

DID YOU KNOW?

Calgary is the largest city in Alberta. It's also Canada's third most densely populated city, behind Toronto in first place and Montréal in second. Edmonton is fifth, just behind Ottawa. Calgary used to be the hub of the province's agriculture; now it's the hub of the oil patch.

Nicknames the Nub of Truth

Edmonton is affectionately called the "City of Potholes" by local residents, but the PR slogans presented to outsiders are "City of Champions," "Shopping Centre Capital of Canada," "Gateway to the North" and "Canada's Festival City."

Calgary's Nickname

Calgary used to be called "Sandstone City," because, errm, sandstone is very easily found in the vicinity, but today, it's called "Cowtown" by Albertans, but the city council wants its new moniker, "Heart of the New West," to be used.

DID YOU  **KNOW?**

The United Way raises more money per person in Calgary than anywhere else in Canada.

Full of Eastern Promise—in the West

Calgary's Chinatown is bigger than any other on the prairies and second only to Vancouver in the West, which is also the biggest in both Canada and North America.

Well Read
Edmonton's public library system has the highest circulation figures in Canada. There are 300 libraries in Alberta.

 Edmonton is home to the largest telephone museum in the world.

Let's Call it Quits?
Both Edmonton and Calgary have spectacular indoor gardens displaying plants from all over the world, from all sorts of climates. Edmonton's is to be found in the four glass pyramids of the Muttart Conservatory, and Calgary's blossom at the downtown Devonian Gardens.

It's Still not Over...
If you take a look at Alberta's cultural scene, the two cities are still fighting it out...

FESTIVAL OFFERINGS

Here's a sampling of what's on offer in both cities in an average year. With more than 40 festivals in Edmonton and similar fare on offer in Calgary, you'll be too busy getting cultured to care.

Edmonton's Major Festivals

☞ Canadian Birkebeiner Ski Festival: Nearly 2000 participate in the cross-country ski festival

☞ Local Heroes International Screen Festival: Independent movies from Canada and the world

- ☛ Comedy Arts Festival: Stand-up, theatre, music, visual arts and clowning
- ☛ Edmonton International Airshow: Airplane acrobatics
- ☛ Dreamspeakers Festival: Aboriginal culture through the arts
- ☛ Northern Alberta International Children's Festival: Acts from around the world performing theatre, music, dance, storytelling and puppetry
- ☛ The Works Art and Design Festival: 1000 artists in over 70 exhibits
- ☛ Whyte Avenue Artwalk: Visual artists display on the street
- ☛ Edmonton Street Performers Festival: World class magicians, clowns, jugglers, mime artists, musicians and comics
- ☛ River City Shakespeare Festival: Shakespeare plays in open-air theatre
- ☛ Klondike Days: Dress up and go back to the 1890s Klondike Gold Rush for concerts, pancake breakfasts, shows and food
- ☛ Edmonton Heritage Festival: A multicultural celebration of food, crafts, dance and song—one of the biggest in Canada
- ☛ Fringe Festival: The largest and longest-running "Fringe" in North America, with over 1500 performers
- ☛ Cariwest: Caribbean parade, performances and music
- ☛ Edmonton Folk Music Festival: Folk, blues, worldbeat and pop artists perform in one of the world's biggest folk music festivals
- ☛ Symphony Under the Sky: Music by the Edmonton Symphony Orchestra in an outdoor amphitheatre
- ☛ Edmonton International Film Festival: Independent film and video
- ☛ Canadian Finals Rodeo: The best rodeo competitors from the Canadian professional rodeo season
- ☛ Farmfair International: Annual agricultural fair

Calgary Events

When you get bored in Edmonton, you could spend another year doing all these things in Calgary. Or vice versa. In fact, some of the events in both cities are remarkably similar.

- PlayRites: New works by Canada's hottest playwrights
- Canada's Cowboy Festival: Do all things cowboy and learn about the area's heritage
- WineFest: An annual festival of wine presenting 250 types to taste
- Funny Fest: Stand-up and improv in western Canada's largest comedy festival
- Spruce Meadows Tournament: Showcase of the world's best equestrian competitions
- Calgary International Childrens' Festival: Hundreds of children's performers, plays, exhibits and clowns
- Ignite! Calgary's Next Generation Arts Festival: Annual theatre festival featuring emerging artists
- Aboriginal Awareness Week: Celebration of all things First Nations
- Calgary International Jazz Festival: Jazz from all over the world played all over the city
- Calgary Exhibition and Stampede: Calgary's premier event of exhibits, rodeo, chuckwagon races and fireworks
- Calgary Folk Music Festival: Week-long party of 40 acts on four stages
- Shady Grove Bluegrass and Old Tyme Music Festival: Celebration of old-time music from days gone by
- Calgary Country Music Week: Country music's best
- Artcity Festival and ArtWalk: Architecture and design exhibitions and lectures
- Calgary International Film Festival: Diverse films from Canada and the world

- Wordfest: Writers gather to show off talents and tricks of the trade—one of Canada's hottest literary events
- Banff Festival of Mountain Films: Meeting of filmmakers, film lovers and movie stars
- Calgary International Piano Competition: World-class competition for pianists held every four years

Albertans are Canada's second-highest spenders on sports, performing arts, recreation and entertainment. Ontario residents spend the most. Albertans also rank highest (per person) for private sector donations to the performing arts than anywhere else in Canada.

Each Canadian drinks an average of 10 Bloody Caesars a year, about 310 million total to be exact, making it the nation's single most popular cocktail. It was invented by Calgary bartender Walter Chell, who simply added "clam nectar" to an ordinary Bloody Mary, which consists of vodka and tomato juice. A California juice company caught on to the recipe, made Clamato juice available commercially, and then the rest of Canada caught on quickly after that.

If It's the Last Thing You Do...

Did you know that the Canadian Death Race, an extreme running and cycling event that goes through mountain ranges near Grande Cache, is an annual event that draws competitors from around the world? It could kill you, because the course is 125 kilometres long, covers three mountain summits and over 5000 metres of elevation change as well as the crossing of a major river at the spectacular Hell's Gates canyon at the confluence of the Smoky and Sulphur Rivers.

EARLY EMPORIUMS

The First Store in Alberta

Montréaler Peter Pond opened the first shop as a trading post 50 kilometres from Lake Athabasca in 1778.

The First Supermarket in Canada

When Henry Marshall Jenkins stocked the shelves of his Calgary "Groceteria" in 1918, the shop became the first self-serve store of its kind in the country.

First One-Stop Shop

The claim to being the oldest shopping centre in the West is held by a store in Lundbreck—the slogan is still painted on the storefront.

MALL MANIA

More Space to Shop

As a result of the oil boom that ended in 1992, Edmonton has 17 major malls, with a combined total of 1.3 million m² of floor space. That's 1.5 m² of enclosed retail space for every man, woman and child—more than any other large city in Canada. By contrast, Vancouver and Toronto have but 0.7 m² of mall per capita and Montreal 0.5 m².

Big Spenders

The province's shoppers spent approximately 20% more dollars above the national average from 1998 to 2003. In 2004, a total of over $43 billion was spent in the province, putting it at the top of Canadian retail sales per capita, with each Albertan spending an average of $12,000 per year, compared to the second-highest per capita spenders, Nova Scotians, who each fork out $10,100 annually.

 Alberta has no provincial retail sales tax, which could explain why there's so much retail therapy going on.

Canada's Largest Shopping Centre

The award goes to West Edmonton Mall (WEM). It held the record for being the World's Biggest Mall from its opening in 1981 until 2004. The crown was lost to the Golden Resources Mall, Beijing, a monster 560,000 m² in size, which provides jobs for 20,000 workers and houses 1000 stores, compared to WEM's 800 stores and 492,000 m² (the equivalent area of 48 city blocks).

Chinese Shopping Colossus
By 2005, China's scramble to make up for all that lost shopping time has resulted in yet another mall bigger than WEM, the South China Mall, in Beijing—530,000 m^2.

DID YOU KNOW?

The Mall of America in Bloomington, Minnesota, is the world's most visited mall, with 35 million people doing retail therapy every year. WEM claims 21 million visitors per year, seven times the population of Alberta.

West Edmonton Mall Still Amazes

It would take three full 24-hour days to visit all of WEM's 800 stores for just five minutes each.

WEM employs someone whose sole responsibility is changing bulbs in the mall's 325,000 light fixtures.

The Fantasyland Hotel at WEM has one of the highest occupancy rates in Canada.

In the 15 years up to 2001, shoppers spent $8.9 billion at WEM—the equivalent of every Albertan spending $3000 per year.

WEM's World Records

- The world's largest indoor theme park
- The world's tallest permanent indoor bungee jump—43 metres
- The world's largest parking lot
- The biggest triple-loop indoor roller coaster in the world. Riders can experience speeds of 100 kilometres per hour and a G-force of 5.2. (Astronauts experience a G-force of just 3 during an average space shuttle launch.)

But Hold on Tight or You Might Fall Out

Shoulder bars or lap bars on roller coasters are now manda-
tory all over the world because of an accident on WEM's
Schwarzkopf (Mindbender) roller coaster. On June 14, 1986,
three people were killed and one seriously injured when they
fell from a car at the top of the loop and landed on the concrete floor below. The accident was caused by a wheel assembly that sheared off the last car. Tragically, the train didn't
have enough speed to complete the loop. The height from
the top of the loop to the floor is just shorter than the Statue
of Liberty, which stands 46.5 metres from the top of the base
to the tip of the torch.

☛ **Safety bars on all loopers**. The ride was closed for 14 months
   while an inquiry was conducted. When the roller coaster
   reopened, it had been modified under the new rules to have
   shorter trains and over-the-shoulder restraints. The rules now
   apply to all traverse loop rides like WEM's Mindbender.

EDUCATION

Term Starts

Alberta's first school was started in Morley in 1874 by two missionary brothers named McDougall. The first teacher was Andrew Sibbald. Alberta's first public school district was established in 1881.

 The first dedicated educational building in Alberta, the Edmonton School, opened on January 3, 1882, directly east of the present-day McKay Avenue School on 104 Street and 99 Avenue, now the Archives and Museum of Edmonton Public Schools.

Mennonites Win Right to Freedoms

In the town of Linden, the Mennonite community took their children out of the local public school and put them into a school of their own because they wanted to teach their own religious beliefs. But the teachers weren't registered, so every parent and child could have legally been charged with truancy. The case went to court in 1978, and the Mennonites won in a landmark case that established both the right to freedom of religious expression and the freedom of individual choice in a child's education.

 One of the world's most prestigious art schools is the Banff Centre School of Fine Arts.

 DID YOU KNOW?

In 2003, Albertans were among the best-educated people in North America.

Certainly Certified

Sixty-five percent of all Albertans aged 25 to 64 reported holding a post-secondary education certificate, diploma or university degree. Nova Scotia, BC and Ontario come in close at just one or two percentage points behind. New Brunswick has the lowest education levels, with approximately 55% of the population educated to at least post-secondary level.

Great Graduates
A whopping 81.5% of Alberta's workforce has at least a high school diploma—one of the highest percentages in the country.

DID YOU KNOW?

The province has the highest number of engineers per capita—two out of every 100 employed Albertans.

Overall Genius
In 2003, 15-year-old Alberta students performed, on average, better overall in mathematics, reading and science than their counterparts in the rest of the country, the U.S. and even the rest of the world.

Mathematical High

Out of 41 countries and Canada's provinces, Alberta scored second highest in mathematics and reading, and fourth highest in science.

Big Spender
Alberta was the third-highest provincial spender on education. In 2003, the government spent nearly $2300 per person, just a few dollars less than Saskatchewan, which came in second, but substantially less than Newfoundland and Labrador, which spent $250 more per person than any other province.

DID YOU KNOW?

Alberta operates its own government education TV network.
The only other provinces to do so are Québec, BC and Ontario.

Lots to Learn

Alberta's publicly funded post-secondary education system has
a total of 24 institutions:

- ☛ Four universities, including the University of Alberta in
  Edmonton (Canada's second largest), as well as institutions in
  Calgary, Lethbridge and Athabasca
- ☛ 14 public colleges
- ☛ Three publicly funded private university colleges
- ☛ Two technical institutes
- ☛ Six hospital-based schools of nursing
- ☛ Approximately 1600 public schools (grades 1 to 12)

HALE AND HEARTY

Long Live Albertans!

People in the province live the third longest of all Canadians, to an average of 79 years, which is two years less than British Columbians, and one less than those living in Ontario. Québecois live to around 78.5 years. Manitoba has the second shortest life expectancy, leaving Newfoundland and Labrador with the lowest life expectancy of around 77.7 years.

Health on Board

The first Municipal Board of Health in Alberta was established in Edmonton in 1892.

The Commonwealth's first municipal hospital was also born in Alberta—some say it was in Mannville, others claim one for Medicine Hat in 1889. Whichever was first, Alberta still wins.

Healthy Workers

Capital Health was Edmonton's single largest employer in 2005.

DID YOU KNOW?

More babies survive their first few years of life in Alberta than all the other Canadian provinces.

Different Strokes for Different Folks

Causes of death differ across the country. The Yukon is the least likely place to die of a stroke, but it's the most likely place to die young in an accident.

Here's a table of what is most likely to cut your life short depending on where you live:

PROVINCIAL COMPARISON OF POTENTIAL YEARS OF LIFE LOST TO DIFFERENT DISEASES (1996)

	TOTAL	CANCER	ACCIDENTS	SUICIDE	RESPIRATORY	HEART DISEASE	STROKE	OTHER
Alberta	3943	1009	963	529	129	492	86	735
Nfld	3721	1152	759	224	77	663	110	737
PEI	3687	1189	829	188	144	642	138	557
Nova Scotia	3983	1264	860	367	147	592	64	689
New Brunswick	3736	1126	758	394	77	589	82	711
Québec	4032	1192	735	660	108	521	98	717
Ontario	3453	1079	601	284	110	475	93	810
Manitoba	4066	1147	936	351	140	546	121	824
Saskatchewan	4203	1086	964	508	161	523	82	879
British Columbia	3986	960	828	279	102	385	75	1357
Yukon	4742	775	1788	457	86	559	0	1078
Northwest Territories	7695	1479	2309	1480	370	481	269	1308

Note: "Potential years of life lost" is a public health measure used to indicate the contribution of different diseases to mortality before age 70.

The Fat Cats Get Fatter...
According to the 1996 National Population Health Survey, one-third of Albertans over age 20 were classified as overweight, 10.3% were obese and 1.6% as morbidly obese.

...and Fatter
In 2003, the percentages were even worse: 39.7% of Albertans were overweight, 14.3% were obese and 3.2% were morbidly obese.

Percent of Population Aged 20 to 64 Reported as Being Overweight in 2004

(As measured by Body Mass Index: weight in kilograms/[height in metres, squared])

Canada 29%

Alberta 30%

British Columbia. 27%

Ontario 29%

Québec 27%

Manitoba 35%

Saskatchewan. 36%

Prince Edward Island. 37%

Nova Scotia 38%

Newfoundland. 39%

New Brunswick. 42%

ALCOHOL, TOBACCO, DRUGS AND GAMBLING

No Drinks Please, We're Albertans

On July 21, 1915, Alberta's all-male electorate voted 61% in favour of Prohibition, and it lasted until abolished across Canada in 1924—and everyone has been making up for that dry patch ever since.

Totally Sloshed

In 2004, Albertans spent a total of $1,560,353 on booze, about $614 per person: $293 on beer, $126 on wine and $195 on spirits.

Hot Toddy
The biggest drinkers in Canada are the coldest: Yukon comes out on top, with the Northwest Territories and Nunavut combined coming in second.

DID YOU KNOW?

Québec, thanks to its *racines françaises*, is the only province where wine is more popular than spirits.

Most of Us Like to Have a Tipple

Eighty percent of Albertans age 15 and older consume alcohol.

But It Can Get Out of Hand

An estimated 8% of the population are frequent, heavy drinkers, 3.5% of Albertans are alcoholics and 13% of Alberta students in grades 7 to 12 knock back alcohol at hazardous or harmful levels.

Life Up in Smoke

On July 1, 2005, Alberta joined 10 out of 13 provinces and territories to ban smoking in public places. So, if you want to smoke inside a public building, you'll have to move to the Yukon or Québec.

Constant Killer

In 2004, tobacco use killed approximately 3400 Albertans. In fact, tobacco use was responsible for more deaths than traffic collisions, HIV/AIDS, murders, suicides and illicit drug use combined.

DID YOU KNOW?

Currently, 20% of Albertans age 15 and older are smokers, but the rate among young adults is much higher, at 31%.

Lay Your Bets, Please

Eighty-two percent of adults gamble, and approximately 5% of Albertans age 18 and older experience moderate to severe addiction and financial problems as a result.

Gamblers in Training

In Alberta, 41% of students gamble, and 9.5% have gambling problems.

BOFFINS, GEEKS AND WHIZ-KIDS

Not surprisingly, in the land where oil, cows and agri-business lead the pack, Albertan inventions and patents have most often been in the same fields.

Hot High-Tech Research

The Alberta Research Council (ARC), established in 1921 in Edmonton, is the largest provincial research organization in Canada, with 400 employees.

Squeezing Out the Last Drop of Oil

It was at the ARC that Dr. Tawfik Nasr discovered how to squeeze more bitumen out of the vast reserves of the province's oil sands by improving the old method of "Steam Assisted Gravity Drainage" (SAGD). The SAGD process, in use since the 1980s, extracts oil from the sand by steaming it. The heat renders the bitumen less viscous, and it drains away from the sand. But this takes a lot of water. Dr. Nasr's new technique adds a solvent that reduces the amount of both water and energy required by half, as well as increasing the yield of oil by nearly 20%. The discovery has given the industry a new lease on life.

Cow Dung Gas

The ARC was also instrumental in the invention of an "integrated manure utilization system." The process recovers biogas (methane) from the mountains of manure produced by livestock feedlots. It was invented by Vegreville's Kotelko family, who own one of the largest feedlot operations in Alberta, capable of holding 36,000 cattle at any one time.

The Buzz of Innovation

In the mid-1960s, Dr. Gordon Hobbs domesticated a wild leaf-cutter bee to pollinate alfalfa crops. He did it at the Lethbridge Research Centre, which is Canada's oldest and largest federal agricultural research facility—100 years old in 2006. Today, Alberta is a leading producer of alfalfa pellets, which cows find particularly tasty, while people prefer the live sprouted version.

Frost-Free Nose Pump

This little wonder was invented in 2002 by Jim and Jackie Anderson of Rimbey. Simply put, it's a hose that pumps water only when a cow pushes down on a lever, which ensures the cow gets to have a drink, even in sub-zero temperatures when water in an ordinary trough would normally freeze. The pump is now used all over North America, wherever there are lots of cows and freezing temperatures.

Slaughtering Site Slap Bang in the Middle of Town

The University of Alberta Farm in Edmonton has a couple of weird claims to fame. The 162-hectare farm, located near an upscale neighbourhood on the south side of town, is one of the largest research facilities of its type in a major urban centre and has fought off endless offers from property developers since its inception in 1915. But would you fancy being neighbours with the poultry facility, where scientists and students conduct specialized and unique research into "micro-slaughter"? It may be the only unit of its kind in North America, but it's one of those places that sounds screechingly noisy to live beside.

THE FUTURE BUZZ

When the oil runs out, the industries of the future will be those researching medical miracles and bio-technology, nanotechnology and communications. And the proof is already in the pharmaceutical pudding...

DID YOU KNOW?

There are 50 bio-technology companies across the province, and 40 of them are in Edmonton.

CV Technologies, based in Edmonton, invented Cold-FX. Today, it's the number-one-selling cold and flu product in Canada, generating sales of $21 million per year.

Lasers Let Loose on Limbless

Until recently, amputees and people who lost their limbs would have a cast made from which a prosthetic would be moulded. But this system can't tell the difference between sensitive areas of skin or harder areas of bone, so there was no way of alleviating extremely painful pressure points in the artificial limb. British-born Calgarian George Clynch solved the problem in 1974 with a system of lasers and software that create comfy custom-made prosthetics.

Calgary Cure for Cancer?

In 1998, Dr. Patrick Lee of the University of Calgary developed a reo-virus (respiratory enteric orphan virus) that may be able to treat up to two-thirds of cancers, which currently account for one in four deaths. The technique involves injecting tumours with a reo-virus, which occurs naturally in humans. Promising results indicate that the reo-virus replicates and continues to kill certain cancer cells until they are obliterated. So far, the technique works on mice.

Done with Diabetes

The "Edmonton Protocol" is the name given to a revolutionary procedure used to treat type 1 diabetes, which is usually controlled by insulin injections. The new treatment was developed by Dr. James Shapiro and Dr. Jonathon Lakey at the University of Alberta. The procedure takes islet cells from the pancreas of a healthy donor (the pancreas is the organ that creates insulin), which are then introduced into the liver of a diabetic patient. Between 50% and 70% of the operations result in a patient successfully producing their own insulin. But recent evidence shows that the effectiveness of the transplant cells deteriorates over time. Extensive research is underway to try and improve the longevity of the procedure.

DID YOU  KNOW?

Fifteen percent of North Americans and 25% of First Nations suffer from diabetes.

A Big Role in the World of the Very Small

Nano is the Greek word for "dwarf," but the future of scientific advance is predicted to be massive in the field of nanotechnology. And the biggest hitter, the National Institute of Nanotechnology, was established in 2001 in Edmonton, a partnership between the University of Alberta and the National Research Council.

DID YOU  KNOW?

Nanotechnology is the atom-by-atom design and fabrication of tiny structures, typically measuring 1 to 100 nanometres, which have powerful applications in medicine and biotechnology, in energy and the environment and in computing and telecommunications.

But Less Costs More
The total budget for equipping the Institute is more than $40 million; $3.5 million is being spent on one "transmission electron microscope" alone, pricey because it's the first instrument of its kind in the world to use electron holography!

Anti-Bacterial Silver Plaster Fuses Nano- and Biotechnology
Fort Saskatchewan researcher Dr. Robert Burrell developed a technique of coating medical dressings with a nano-layer of silver just one micron thick. (A human hair is 80 microns thick.) Silver has long been known to be anti-microbial, but Burrell's new technique overcame the problem that silver becomes ineffective when it contacts chlorine on human skin. The dressings are now used to treat serious burn victims and are also available commercially as wound coverings.

OTHER ALBERTAN DISCOVERIES AND INVENTIONS

Sucrose Synthesizer

The first scientist to synthesize sucrose (sugar) was Dr. Raymond Lemieux, who was born in Lac La Biche and studied, then later taught, at the University of Alberta. At the time, in 1953, the discovery was considered the apex of organic chemistry. Since then, the study of complex carbohydrates (oligosaccharides) and Dr. Lemieux's work has led to made many other ground-breaking discoveries in the field of antibiotics and immunology.

Safety Suitcase of the Sea Spawned on the Prairies

Strange that Claresholm, which is landlocked and thousands of miles away from any ocean, was the birthplace of the "Flotation Suitcase." The inventor, John Edlund, created the contraption, which could also be worn as a helmet. Now there's fashion statement. If you hit the water and happen to stay afloat long enough to open the bag, there's a chance you might be able to unfold the suit's legs and arms and climb in. Now there's another fashion statement. Life preserved at the cost of dignity.

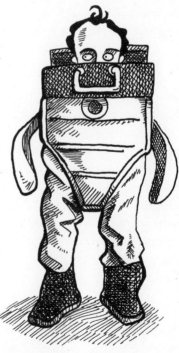

Silver Turns to Gold

Albertans Thomas Etsell and Wasyl Kunda together created a host of brand new techniques to mine and refine metal ores that later set industry benchmarks for nickel, cobalt and copper. They also patented a process in 1992 that recovers two-thirds of the silver used in processing photographic prints. They sold their invention for a small fortune and helped keep the environment clean.

Old and New Techniques Cleaning Up Drinking Water

Alberta inventor Dr. David Manz created a water filtration system in 1993 that now provides drinking water to countries in the Third World that couldn't otherwise afford it. The technique is based on slow sand filtration, which is a low-tech process first invented 170 years ago. It takes a long, long time but requires no power—perfect for poor countries.

The Eyes of the Canadarm

The man who co-designed the Canadarm, Lloyd Pinkey, was an engineering and physics graduate of the University of Alberta. Pinkey also designed the Space Vision System, which calculates and displays the location, orientation and speed at which objects are moving in relation to the Canadarm and the space shuttle/station upon which it is mounted. Today, this data is being fed to the Canadarm 2, allowing it to move objects with such extreme accuracy that the arm is being used to construct the International Space Station in orbit and from within the space station itself.

Alberta has the only animal forensics lab in the world. The Neil Crawford Centre finds out exactly how animals died, mostly as a way of catching poachers.

Animal Crime Scene Investigators

Alberta leads the world in the new field of animal forensics. Dr. Curtis Strobeck, professor of biological sciences at the University of Alberta, is refining methods used by cops to track down criminals into leading edge techniques used by rangers to sniff out animals. In a recent case, Dr. Strobeck proved that a grizzly bear sow, which was shot dead by rangers on suspicion of having torn apart six tents at a Lake Louise campground, was actually innocent. DNA samples of hair taken from the shredded tents were finally proven to be those of another sow, which had been recently captured but was later released into BC.

Bear-Proof Bin

The number of problem bears increases depending on their chances of finding human leftovers to snack on. A solution was found in a bear-proof bin designed by a Calgary company, Haul-All. The bin is strong enough to withstand a bear's force and has a heavy lid that shuts tight with a mechanism that bear paws cannot penetrate, but humans can open easily. Since the installation of the bins, the number of problem bear incidents in Alberta's national parks has declined dramatically.

Fragile Fossils No Longer

Dr. Paul Johnston, a curator at the Royal Tyrrell Museum in Drumheller, invented a solution to the problem of identifying fossils so intricate and delicate they would break up before he could extract them from the rock they were embedded in. The first step is to dissolve the calcium carbonate fossil only, in acid, leaving behind an impression of the fossil in the rock. The empty space is then filled with plastic that sets rock hard. The rock itself is then dissolved, leaving an exact plastic replica of the fossil. Voila! A synthetic substitute, enabling new areas of investigation into rocks previously thought to be impenetrable.

Cutting Back Radio Highs

In the early days of radio, a station could have its frequency
shifted or get completely knocked off the airwaves if it broadcast
too much noise—even inevitable things like lisps that were
too loud or sopranos hitting high notes. So Edward Jordan,
Edmonton-based CKUA Radio's first control-room operator,
came up with a device called the "Peak Limiter" which modulat-
ed any extreme racket. The invention was high-tech for its
time—1936—and was soon keeping almost all the stations in
North America successfully on the air.

Ships Built of Ice

"Habbakuk" was the Old Testament name given to a project so
ambitious it was biblical, in this case, a top secret WWII project.
The aim? To build ships. Out of ice! The idea was the brainchild
of the British government hoping to build cheap, icy aircraft
carriers (admittedly ice *is* cheaper than steel) that were attack-
resistant and unsinkable. Canucks have a lot of ice, as well as
perfectly chilly places to test prototypes, so the National
Research Council in Alberta was invited to join the experiment.
The project was shelved as the war drew to a close, so a frozen
ship was never made, but scientists did learn loads about the
properties of ice.

EMPLOYMENT

The Jobless Few

Alberta's average unemployment rate of 4.9% was the lowest among the provinces, well below the national average of 7.3% for the period 1998 to 2003.

Working Albertans are on average 31 years of age, three years younger than the national average.

Lots of Jobs in Alberta

There were 42,700 more jobs in Alberta in 2004 than in the previous year. Alberta's employment rate was 70.2% in 2003, compared to the Canadian average of 62.7%. Newfoundland and Labrador had the lowest employment rate, at only 50%.

More women work outside the home in Alberta—60%—than in any other Canadian province.

Leading in Sales

More Albertans are employed in sales than any other occupation. So if you want a job selling something, Alberta's the place to be, but if it's high culture you're after, it's going to be really competitive.

EMPLOYMENT BY OCCUPATION IN ALBERTA (2004)

Occupation	'000
Sales and service occupations	422.3
Trades, transport and equipment operator and related occupations	313.4
Business, finance and administrative occupations	310.7
Management occupations	145.3
Natural and applied sciences and related occupations	127.0
Occupations in social science, education, government service and religion	120.7
Occupations unique to primary industry	117.5
Health occupations	91.3
Occupations unique to processing, manufacturing and utilities	69.3
Occupations in art, culture, recreation and sport	40.4
All occupations	**1757.9**

STANDARD OF LIVING

Money in my Pocket

From 1998 to 2003, Albertans had the highest average rate of personal disposable income (money to spend after taxes) than people in other provinces—nearly 14% above the national average, at $33,083 per person.

DID YOU  KNOW?

Alberta has the best standard of living in Canada—118% of the national average. Ontario is the only other province with a better standard than the rest, at 108%. All other provinces are lower, with PEI the lowest at 70% of the national average.

The Poor Don't Earn Much
At $5.90 per hour, Alberta used to have the lowest minimum wage in the country—90 cents an hour below the national average. It went up to $7 in September 2005, the same as Manitoba's—now both provinces have the fourth-highest minimum wage.

Wages Aren't Going Up Either
Wages have remained stagnant in the last decade. Measured in 2001 constant dollars, adjusted to correct for inflation, the average weekly wage in Alberta in 1993 was $676.79. In 2003, it was $676.14.

Some of the Lowest Welfare Rates in the Nation
Monthly allowances for housing and shelter are on average $164 less than the average rental property. According to the Edmonton Social Planning Council, Alberta's current welfare payments fall 42% short of the actual cost of goods and services that an average family needs each month.

Single Parents Poorest

Alberta provides the worst level of support for single moms or dads among all the provinces—the sum given, 48%, isn't even half the amount considered as the poverty line benchmark. Newfoundland and Labrador provides the most support, at 71% of the poverty line.

Rich Getting Richer and the Poor Poorer

The following table shows that of all the provinces, Alberta's poorest 10% of the population are the poorest in the whole country, with an average wealth of only $5,314. Alberta also has the second biggest gap between the wealth of the richest 10% and the poorest 10%—only BC has a larger gap. Income is distributed most evenly in the Atlantic provinces.

WEALTH OF THE RICHEST AND POOREST BY PROVINCE (2003)

	AVERAGE WEALTH OF RICHEST 10%	AVERAGE WEALTH FOR POOREST 10% () = MINUS	GAP BETWEEN RICHEST AND POOREST
BC	$1,378,534	($8,126)	$1,386,660
Ontario	$1,088,364	($7,096)	$1,095,460
Prairies	$1,135,499	($5,655)	$1,141,154
Alberta	**$1,311,401**	**($5,314)**	**$1,316,715**
CANADA	$1,059,423	($7,110)	$1,066,533
Québec	$868,517	($7,067)	$ 875,584
Atlantic	$604,669	($8,227)	$ 612,896

Lowest Rate of Unionization in the Country

Only 25% of the province's workforce is unionized, compared to a national average of about 33%. The unions say this has more to do with harsh employment laws than workers' desires to be unionized.

University Costs Going Nuts

From 1992 to 2002, Alberta had the highest increase in university tuition fees (161%) among all the provinces and the second-highest increase in college tuition fees (293%).

DID YOU KNOW?

The price of a house in Calgary or Edmonton is approximately 30% to 40% less than a home in Toronto or Vancouver.

Low Gas Taxes

At 9.0 cents per litre in 2005, Alberta has the lowest gasoline tax rate among the provinces, 2.5 cents per litre below Manitoba, the second lowest province. Indeed, over the last 15 years, Calgary and Edmonton have had the lowest gasoline prices in Canada. Well, most of it is produced just up the road, so that's no great shakes really, is it?

DID YOU KNOW?

Before deregulation, Albertans paid among the lowest utilities rates in the country. Now they pay the highest.

Not the Cheapest Place to Live

Comparing major cities across Canada, the cost of a basket of essential goods and services (such as food, utilities, household operations, transportation, health/personal care, recreation and tobacco/alcohol products) that costs $100 in Edmonton, will set you back $80 to $90 in Montréal, Winnipeg, Halifax, Regina and Toronto. The good news is that the same basket would cost about $3 more in Vancouver, $8 more in Saint John, New Brunswick, and $29 more in St. John's, Newfoundland.

THE BUSINESS OF MAKING MONEY

Good for Business

Alberta cities are among the most cost-competitive in the world according to a 2004 analysis by KPMG of the relative costs of doing business in 63 cities in 11 countries in North America, Europe and the Asia-Pacific region. (Canada ranked number one overall for cost effectiveness.) Edmonton ranked second, and Calgary ranked seventh.

The average growth in wealth generated by Alberta's businesses from 1998 to 2003 was the fastest of any province in Canada. The actual number of businesses in Alberta also increased by 2% in 2004, the strongest growth of all the provinces.

Headquarters Haven

Calgary has the highest number of business headquarters per person than any other Canadian city. The city boasts approximately eight head offices for every 100,000 persons. It could be called "little Houston" because most of these are oil companies— actually 85% of all of Canada's energy HQs. Regina comes in at second place with about 4.5 HQs, Vancouver and Montréal with just over two and Edmonton with just under two.

Loads of Money

Calgary tycoon Murray Edwards is thought to be the richest man in Alberta. His net worth was pegged at $757 million in 2003, *before* oil prices soared. Edwards co-owns Canadian Natural Resources Ltd., one of the world's largest independent oil and gas companies, worth $13 billion in 2003. He is the CEO and director of many other companies as well as being part-owner of the Calgary Flames and a majority owner of Resorts of the Canadian Rockies, which owns the Lake Louise Ski Area and eight other ski resorts.

Alberta's Biggest Businesses

Energy . . . . $19.7 billion

Industrial and consumer products manufacturing $17.8 billion

Agriculture and food processing . . . . $10.0 billion

Information and communications technology . . . . . $8.7 billion

Building and construction . . . . $6.3 billion

Forestry . . . . $5.5 billion

Tourism. . . . . $4.6 billion

OIL, GAS AND COAL

What's Tops?
The number one export in Alberta is… (duh!) Energy! Oil, gas and coal.

Saudis Oilier than Canucks

Canada is second only to Saudi Arabia in total oil reserves, and 95% of the oil is found in Alberta. But all the Saudis have to do is find it, drill a hole and the dollars spurt out. The Canadian reserves are held in sands that are sticky, heavy and difficult to process, so even though there are 1.6 trillion barrels of bitumen, only 175 billion barrels are currently thought to be recoverable.

Alberta produces about 81% of Canada's natural gas, 67% of its crude oil, 49% of its coal and possesses all of its oil sands.

World's Largest Oil Sands Development

Top of the list is Alberta's Suncor and Syncrude oilsands plants in Fort McMurray. Huge money—$87 billion worth of investment—is due to be pumped into oil sands projects from 1996 to 2016.

Canada's Major Oil Pipelines Cut Through Alberta

A 9000-mile network of pipelines and terminals takes oil from Edmonton to eastern Canada and the U.S. Great Lakes region. The Trans Mountain Pipeline takes oil mainly from western Alberta to refineries and terminals in the Vancouver area.

DID YOU KNOW?

Alberta is the biggest consumer of energy in Canada, using about 2.5 times the national average per person in 2003. Considering that Canadians consume three times as much energy as Italians, that makes Albertans ghastly gas guzzlers.

"The Road to Nowhere"

This is the nickname given to the Peter Lougheed Bridge, built at Fort McMurray. Originally designed to link up the town to the Alsands oil plant, the plant was never built, and the bridge was abandoned.

Alberta's Oil

- ☛ 62% goes to the U.S. (and fills 5% of the U.S.'s crude oil needs)
- ☛ 24% is used within Alberta
- ☛ 14% goes to the rest of Canada

World Energy Leader

Worldwide, Alberta is the:

- ☛ Ninth-largest oil producer
- ☛ Second-largest natural gas exporter
- ☛ Third-largest natural gas producer

Natural Gas Production in Alberta

In 2001, 141.6 billion m^3 of natural gas were produced, valued at $2.7 billion.

Of the natural gas produced in the province:

- ☛ 16% is sold in Alberta
- ☛ 33% is sold to the rest of Canada
- ☛ 51% is exported to the U.S. (13% of the U.S.'s natural gas needs)

Edmonton Busy Processing

Over half of Canada's petrochemical processors and manufacturers are based in Alberta, predominantly east of Edmonton. The Fort Saskatchewan area is part of the largest industrial area west of Toronto. Petrochemicals are the province's second-largest manufacturing industry, producing over $9.5 billion in 2004.

 Alberta contains 70% of Canada's coal reserves and produces about half of the coal currently mined in the country each year.

Homegrown Power
Alberta-produced coal is used to generate about 80% of Alberta's electricity. In 1998, Alberta mined its 1 billionth tonne of coal.

The value of energy from Alberta's coal reserves is equal to that of the oil sands and crude reserves combined.

Can Coal be Clean?

Alberta's coal contains only a very small amount of sulphur, which makes burning it relatively clean and less polluting compared to other types found elsewhere.

FORESTRY

Tree Replanting

Every year, approximately 23.3 million m³ of the province's forests are harvested and then replenished with 2.2 billion m³ of saplings.

DID YOU KNOW?

Fifty-eight percent of the province's land area is covered by forest.

Chip Off the Old Block

Fifty Alberta mills manufacture products such as lumber, pulp, newsprint, panelboard and secondary wood products. Today, this accounts for $5.5 billion annually, and over three quarters of it are exported.

Hands Off Our Trees!

Twenty-seven percent of Alberta's forests have been designated off limits to resource developers in an effort to protect the environment. Really? Well…

People Power

A Japanese paper company was put under so much pressure from a successful Canadian-wide boycott of their products, that they agreed to stop clearcutting land that was home to the Lubicon Cree tribe. The land rights had been granted to the company by the Alberta government.

THE BUSINESS OF FARMING

History... celebrates the battlefields whereon we meet our death,
but scorns to speak of the plowed fields whereby we thrive;
it knows the names of the king's bastards, but cannot tell us the
origin of wheat. That is the way of human folly.

Jean-Henri Fabre

Flourishing from the Foundations

For the first homesteaders and cowboys, growing food was a
matter of survival. Today, farming and agri-business have grown
into highly industrialized, high-tech industries and still form the
backbone of Alberta's economy.

 DID YOU KNOW?

There are 53,652 farms in Alberta, with approximately 149,000
people living in farm households. Total farmland area in the
province is 21 million hectares. The average farm size is 392.5
hectares.

A Fifth of Federal Farming

Alberta annually accounts for 22% of Canada's total agricultural
production with only 9% of Canada's population. In 2001, total
Alberta farm cash receipts reached $8.3 billion, over $3 billion
of which was generated by the beef/cattle industry.

Biggest Beef

Alberta is the largest producer of beef cattle in Canada, with
about a 67.7% share of market-ready cattle. Ontario comes in
second with 21.2%.

Beef Industry Slaughtered by Mad Cow Disease

The industry suffered terrible losses after the discovery of mad cow disease in one Albertan cow in May 2003. The Americans closed their borders to Alberta beef, and other countries banned imports. With no one wanting to buy beef, the price of a cow plummeted from an average $1500 per head to a mere $15.

Before the Beef Ban

Prior to the worldwide ban on Canadian beef products, Canada was the third largest exporter of beef in the world, after Australia and the United States.

DID YOU  KNOW?

Canadians eat about 14.2 kilograms of beef per person per year. The amount went up about 5% during the mad cow crisis.

Very Costly Cows

Federal and provincial compensation packages to cattle ranchers and beef producers totalled $1.9 billion by the end of 2005, partly to make up for the mass slaughter of 620,000 cattle to reduce the size of the herd and prevent further damage to the industry.

Opening Up Again

The United States reopened its borders to young live Canadian cattle less than 30 months old in March 2005, but still continued to ban trade in beef products from older animals.

The world's largest producer of frozen pyrogies is Edmonton's Heritage Frozen Foods. A traditional pyrogy is a Ukrainian dumpling filled with potato and cheese, sauerkraut or bacon. Nowadays they're stuffed with almost anything.

Word of Mouth

The Big Rock Brewery is Alberta's first successful microbrewery, started by Calgary's Ed McNally in 1984. The beer is so good, it's become a household name in North America even though the company hardly does any advertising.

New Kid on the Block

Alberta's other microbrewery, Maverick, which opened on August 1, 2005, is the newest. Its HQ in downtown Edmonton is open for visitors to watch the brewmeisters at work.

Alberta is the third largest food and beverage producing province in Canada. Food and beverage production is also the province's largest manufacturing sector, which employs 20% of the manufacturing workforce.

In the last decade, Alberta produced about a quarter of the nation's wheat crop, two fifths of the barley and a quarter of the oats.

The Birth of Canola Oil

The term "canola" is a contraction of "Canadian oil." A much more politically correct name than rapeseed, right? Canola is Canada's leading vegetable oil, and Alberta produces one-third of it. Today, over 5 million hectares of Canadian soil are dedicated to canola production, and around 70% is exported to the U.S.

DID YOU  KNOW?

Canada ranks in the top five in the world today as an exporter of alfalfa pellets and alfalfa cubes, and most of those crops are produced in Alberta and Saskatchewan.

 Alberta is Canada's major bison-producing province, with 400 producers. The meat has become *über* trendy because it is low in fat and high in nutrients.

Powerful Prairie Taters

Alberta's first potato chip factory was built in Calgary in 1970 by Old Dutch Foods. Today, Alberta has blossomed into a potato powerhouse with almost 21,000 hectares of land producing 9 billion commercial potatoes annually. Today's taters are seeded from potatoes that were originally brought over by settlers from their homelands.

Prairie Wine!!

Alberta now even has a fruit winery—the Fieldstone Winery in Strathmore was approved in 2005. The province has 250 to 300 fruit and berry growers who currently cultivate 1050 hectares of land in an admittedly short growing season.

Taber Cornfest

Even though sweet corn is almost impossible for humans to digest, it's so sweet and juicy that the town of Taber is devoted to growing it and throwing an annual celebratory festival the last weekend of August.

Marketing Farmers

The Edmonton City Market, established in 1900, was the first of Alberta's farmers' markets—a way for producers to sell directly to consumers. By 1973, there were only four farmers' markets still operating in the whole province, one each in Calgary, Edmonton, Lethbridge and Medicine Hat. Since 1994, between 110 and 120 new markets were cultivated and are now flourishing under the auspices of the Alberta Farmer's Market Association.

Breeding Bulls

The most popular cattle breed in the world is one of the oldest— the Simmental, originally from Switzerland. Its introduction in America began in Alberta in 1967, when a bull called Parisien was let loose on the cows. He and others like him must have done a good job and had a really good time, because today there are more Simmental in North America than any other breed.

 Seed grower Joe Dennis of Leduc invented a peanut butter that's made without peanuts. So anyone with allergies can try NoNuts Golden Peabutter which is made of dry brown peas, canola oil, icing sugar and monoglyceride (sugar) from canola and cottonseed oils.

Sweet Sap Saves on Sugar

In 1992, Warren Bard became the first commercial producer to bottle birch syrup. It was first used as a sugar substitute in the Klondike days when sugar was hard to find.

Designer Eggs

Jeong Sim, a professor of agricultural, food and nutritional science at the University of Alberta, impregnated eggs with omega-3 fatty acids in a process that is secret and covered by a commercial patent. Omega acids, normally found in fish, keep hearts healthy and improve your brain—and most Canadians don't get nearly enough of them.

BUILDING AND CONSTRUCTION

Build It and They Will Come

With so many people moving into the province, they had to live somewhere, and in 2004, construction began on 36,270 new homes in the province.

DID YOU  **KNOW?**

Over 300,000 Alberta residents live in modular or manufactured housing, which accounted for 40% of the rural housing starts in Alberta in 2000.

Building Blocks That Aren't Toys

Alberta's building products industry is one of the largest and strongest in the country, with local production valued at $6.25 billion and exports reaching $1.93 billion in 2001. There are more than 1200 manufacturers of building products in Alberta, and the sector employs over 36,000 people.

INFORMATION IS POWER

Let's Talk About the Future

The future is all about ICT—information, communications and technology industries—which made about $8.7 billion in 2004. And it was the work of a Calgarian that has led some of the way…

Global Computer Language

Did you know that Java, the computer language script used by all computers all over the world to communicate with each other, regardless of the software or hardware they use, was invented by a Calgarian? Wherever there's a computer, chances are Java will be making it work, and it's all thanks to James Gosling, a native Albertan who studied computer science at the University of Calgary.

Alberta Sounds Heard Worldwide

Calgary inventors Dan Lowe and John Lees invented a system called the QSound 3-D Recording System, which is used in a plethora of sound-emitting devices, ranging from TV programs to CDs, as well as audio streamed on the Internet and computer sound cards. Simply put, QSound tricks the brain into thinking that sound is being created in three-dimensional space, so the listener thinks the sound is coming from all sides.

Interactive Smarts

David Martin and Nancy Knowlton of Calgary invented the Smart Board, a device that acts as an all-in-one whiteboard, computer and projector. People anywhere in the world can control the device from the whiteboard, which functions as a giant computer screen and mouse. The board allows people to interact and collaborate in a real-time electronically shared space. So far 100,000 boards have been sold.

DID YOU KNOW?

Albertans are the most connected Canucks when it comes to Internet technology. Just over 60,000 homes have access to the Net. Considering that Canada is the most connected country in the world, that puts Alberta at the top of the table worldwide.

Alberta has the highest number of households in Canada with:

☛ Telephones (99%)
☛ Cellular Phones (51%)
☛ Computers (63%)

Telephone Town

Pincher Creek is home to Crystal Village, where someone put up 13 buildings made out of telephone parts—200,000 insulators and 900 crossarms.

The "Supernet" is Online!

Forty-two hundred government, health, library and education facilities in 429 communities across the province can now get access to broadband Internet at rates subsidized by the provincial government. The first municipality to provide Internet access at its local library was Drayton Valley.

Hello!

Sixty telecommunications companies operate in Alberta. Collectively, they generate more than $5.8 billion a year in revenue and employ more than 17,000 people.

The Call Centre Capital of the World??

Some experts forecast a massive explosion in Alberta's information technology industry—predictions for 2010 suggest 140,000 people will be employed, generating more than $30 billion annually. Although there will be hi-tech, highly paid jobs available, a lot of jobs will be filled by low-paid, well-educated people answering phones and questions in Alberta's blossoming call centre business.

Computer Games

Baldur's Gate and the latest release, *The Jade Empire,* are two of the biggest blockbusters in the world of computer games, and they're made by Edmonton's BioWare. It's one of Alberta's most successful and youngest of a new breed of companies—its 200 employees are mostly under 30 and make a million dollars a year each in profits. In 2003, the company won the prestigious British Academy of Film and Television Arts award for Best PC Game: *Neverwinter Nights.* BioWare was set up in 1995 by two medical doctors who shared an obsession for computer games.

☞ **Kaboom!** In 2005, the company merged with Pandemic (based in L.A. and Brisbane, Australia). BioWare/Pandemic is now one of the world's best-funded and largest independent video game development houses.

More Fun and Games

Edmonton's Grant Skinner was named Canada's best Macromedia Flash developer for a game called *Puki*. (Flash is a program that displays text and images.) The award recognized his creation of the first-ever true 3-D first-person-computer-shooter game. More than a million people played the game online in the first three weeks it was launched in 2005.

Telecommunications Quiz

1) What year was Alberta's first telegraph line installed?
2) Which organization opened the province's first post office?
3) How old was Edmonton's first telephone operator?
4) What was invented in 1920 but wasn't received in Alberta until 1940?

1) 1877
2) The North-West Mounted Police at Fort Macleod.
3) Jennie Lauder was 13 years old.
4) Television broadcasts, and just like most TV today, the pictures were from the U.S.

TRIVIAL POLITICS

Never retreat, never explain, never apologize—get the thing done and let them howl.

Nellie McClung

Provincial Power

Alberta's provincial government is made up of 83 Members of the Legislative Assembly. Alberta has 28 seats (MPs) in the Federal Parliament.

DID YOU  **KNOW?**

Alberta's Legislature building is sitting on quicksand. But the foundations are good.

Quick Clark

Canada's second Albertan Prime Minister, Joe Clark, steered the helm for one of the shortest ever of Canadian Parliaments...only nine months, starting in June 1979. The only other Albertan PM was R.B. Bennett, who served a five-year term starting in 1930.

Youngest and Oldest

Joe Clark was the youngest PM ever to take office, at the age of 39 years, 11 months. The oldest was Sir Charles Tupper, who became PM on May 1, 1896, at the age of 74 years, 10 months.

DID YOU  **KNOW?**

In 1916, Alberta became the third province after Manitoba and Saskatchewan to grant women the right to vote in provincial elections.

Ma'am the Magistrate

Edmonton's Emily Murphy and Alice Jamieson of Calgary became the first female magistrates in the British Empire in 1916.

Another Feisty Political Female

Calgarian social activist Annie Gale became the first woman in the British Empire to serve on a municipal council, in 1917, when she was elected alderman in Calgary. She also served as acting mayor on occasion, another historical first.

First Female MLA

In 1917, temperance activist Louise McKinney became the first woman in the British Empire to sit in a legislature when she won the seat for Claresholm in the Alberta provincial election.

Alberta's Famous Five

This title is affectionately given to the group of women who changed the face of politics in Canada and the Commonwealth. They won the fight to have women declared persons in the eyes of the law and become eligible for election at all levels of politics. They were Alberta's Henrietta Muir Edwards, Nellie McClung, Louise McKinney, Emily Murphy and Irene Parlby.

☛ **Canadian woman not legal.** A woman was not a legal "person" until 1929. The British North America Act (BNA) declared: "Women are persons in matters of pain and penalties, but are not persons in matters of rights and privileges." This prevented women from being elected to the Canadian Senate because of a Supreme Court ruling, which interpreted the law that individuals must be "fit and qualified" to be appointed to a public office—therefore only men were eligible.

☛ **The highest court in the land...over there.** So the Famous Five appealed to the highest court in the Commonwealth, the Privy Council in England, which reached the landmark decision on October 18, 1929, that declared women were to be considered "persons" under the law, and "women are eligible to be summoned and may become Members of the Senate of Canada."

Fifty Years in the Making

But it took another 50 years before Martha Beilish became Alberta's first female senator. Since then, Joyce Fairbairn (who was also the first woman to be appointed Leader of the Government in the Senate), Jean Forest, Elaine McCoy, Claudette Tardif and Thelma Chalifoux (who was the first Métis and first Aboriginal woman senator) are the other Albertan women who have sat on the Senate of Canada.

First Time for First Nations

At a time when First Nations in Alberta didn't even have the right to vote, James Gladstone, the former president of the Indian Association of Alberta, became the first aboriginal appointed to the Canadian Senate in 1958.

DID YOU KNOW?

First Nations were also not defined as "persons" under the 1880 Indian Act. It wasn't until 1960 that they could vote in national elections.

Métis MP

The first Métis to be elected as an MP in Alberta was Mike Cardinal for the Conservatives in 1989.

DID YOU  KNOW?

Women now account for more than one-third of the Canadian Senate's membership, a higher representation than any other legislative assembly in North America.

Female Cabinet Ministers

The first five women to serve in Alberta's provincial cabinet were: Irene Parlby (1921–35), Ethel Wilson (1959–71), Helen Hunley (1971–79), Mary LeMessurier (1979–86) and Connie Osterman (1979–92).

Women Still Have a Long Way to Go

- ☛ Only 13 out of Alberta's 83 MLAs were women in 2005—about 15% female.
- ☛ In 2005, Canada's 38th Parliament had a total of 65 women MPs out of a total of 307, or 21%.
- ☛ Only three MPs out of 28 available seats in Alberta were female, or 11%.
- ☛ The Honourable Helen Hunley was Alberta's first female Lieutenant-Governor of Alberta, serving from 1985–91.

 Richard Gavin Reid (UFA) was the Alberta premier who served the shortest—13 months—and lived the longest, 101 years.

DID YOU  KNOW?

The only Canadian-born Lord Mayor of London, England, was Peter Gadsen, an Albertan born in Mannville.

MISCELLANY

THE MOST POPULAR BABY NAMES IN ALBERTA

BOYS
Ethan, Joshua, Matthew,
Jacob, Logan, Nathan,
Alexander, Ryan, Tyler,
Benjamin

GIRLS
Emma, Emily, Madison,
Sarah, Hannah, Taylor,
Olivia, Jessica, Ella, Hailey

Don't Put the Top Down
It is illegal for women to go topless in Alberta. So, if you want, you can do it next door in Saskatchewan. Two women were acquitted there in 1999 of the "public nuisance" offence of taking their clothes off.

The Divorce Rate in Alberta
Marital breakups went up 357% between 1961 and 2003. Currently just over half of all marriages (51%) end in a breakup.

Biggest Wins in the Same Year
The year 1989 was a big one for big lottery wins in Alberta. Ron and Val Taylor of Killam won $10,372,326.70 in 1989. The third biggest western Canadian win was a trio from Calgary; Ken Brown, Wing Gee and Terry Johnston who won just over $10 million the same year.

Bingo! Boom! Bam! The BIG ONE!
In October 2005, the biggest lottery win in Canadian history, $54.3 million, was scored by a group of 17 workers at a Camrose gas plant. They each got $3.19 million. One woman, Deb Leslie, only entered the consortium that day because she was worried about her farmer-husband's bad harvest. She had to borrow the $20 bucks to play.

10 REASONS OR MORE TO LIVE IN ALBERTA

1. Alberta is Canada's only rat-free province. It's been clean since 1905.

2. The provincial government owns the rights to Alberta's mineral resources, so license fees and taxes on energy companies profits come to provincial coffers. Sorry Ottawa!

3. Alberta has the best overall weather of all the Canadian provinces!

4. Albertans have a lot of fun shopping. They spend more in retail stores than other Canadians. High disposable incomes mean lots of buying power.

5. Albertans have one of the highest rates of fatal car accidents in Canada, which is a really good reason to be a-LIVE in Alberta.

6. Alberta is not only alive and kicking on its 100th birthday, September 1, 2005, it's really going strong—growing faster economically than any other Canadian province.

7. Alberta has a dinosaur named after it: the *Albertosaurus sarcophagus.*

8. Albertans are some of the very smartest people in North America. Nearly two-thirds of the population have a post-secondary qualification.

9. Alberta has a new beer. It's called "Maverick Supreme Lager," first brewed in the summer of 2005 by the Maverick Brewing Co.—Alberta's only destination craft brewery.

10. The commodity of the future could well be clean drinking water, and Alberta has enough of the stuff that it is completely self-sufficient. So drink on! Over 90% of the prairie provinces' potable *eau* comes from Alberta.

11. Alberta has no Provincial Sales Tax. Actually, it doesn't have a provincial general capital tax either, or a payroll tax, nor a machinery and equipment tax. And the province boasts Canada's lowest fuel taxes. That's five reasons in one. Bargain!

12. Alberta is Canada's only debt-free province. Okay, the roads don't get cleared much in winter, and there's never enough health care, but hey, this isn't about politics, it's about lots of oily black stuff that a lot of people are making a lot of money on, and hallelujah, some of it might be coming back to the people who live here.

Still not convinced? Consider this...

13. Would you rather live at the North Pole? It's much colder there than it is here.

14. If Alberta weather was any better, lots of Americans would probably pack their bags and move up here. Then we'd be overcrowded, eh?

15. Alberta is much, much cooler than the Bahamas, which is much too hot. Which is probably why Canada geese never fly anywhere near the place—whether on migration or on holidays.

ABOUT THE AUTHOR

Marina Michaelides

Marina has always been so inquisitive about how the world works, she has never sat still. She was born a twin in London, England, to parents who emigrated there from the island of Cyprus. Marina received her degree in economics and management, and later a post-graduate diploma in communications. She worked as a documentary filmmaker in the UK for a decade, and in between projects, travelled all around the world searching for the meaning of life. Once she found out that it's all about loving the little things, she finally decided to settle down in Edmonton, Alberta. Marina continues to make award-winning documentaries for television, as well as write for magazines and journals…and, often, she loves to ponder the question of why we are here.